Turning Promises into Performance

Turning Promises into Performance

THE MANAGEMENT CHALLENGE OF IMPLEMENTING WORKFARE

Richard P. Nathan

A Twentieth Century Fund Book

COLUMBIA UNIVERSITY PRESS

New York

Excerpt from "The Hollow Men" in *Collected Poems, 1909–1962* by T. S. Eliot, © 1936 by Harcourt Brace Jovanovich, Inc., © 1964, 1963 by T. S. Eliot, reprinted by permission of the publisher.

The Twentieth Century Fund is a research foundation undertaking timely analyses of economic, political, and social issues. Not-for-profit and nonpartisan, the Fund was founded in 1919 and endowed by Edward A. Filene.

Columbia University Press
New York   Chichester, West Sussex
Copyright © 1993 The Twentieth Century Fund
All rights reserved

Library of Congress Cataloging-in-Publication Data

Nathan, Richard P.
Turning promises into performance : the management challenge of
implementing workfare / Richard P. Nathan.
p.   cm.
"A Twentieth Century Fund book."
Includes index.
ISBN 0–231–07962–1   ISBN 0–231–07963–X (pbk.)
1. Welfare recipients—Employment—United States.   2. Public
welfare administration—United States.   I. Title.
HV95.N28   1933
351.84'5—dc20
92–42821
CIP

Casebound editions of Columbia University Press books are printed on
permanent and durable acid-free paper.
Printed in the United States of America

c 10 9 8 7 6 5 4 3 2 1

For Mary with love

Contents

Foreword

God must love the poor because he made so many of them."
Allowing for the possibility that "she" might be equally appropriate,
the old saying retains a certain relevance; perhaps, for example, it can
be used to excuse, if not explain, why we "made" so many more of
them in God's country, that is, in the United States, in recent years.
Today, 14.2 percent of U.S. residents, more than 35.7 million people,
live in poverty, surviving on incomes under $13,924 a year.

This growth in the number of the poor—the number is the highest
since 1964—has not been accompanied, despite the great income gains
by the richest among us, by a significant overall increase in the majority's share of the economic pie. In fact, in 1989 the average worker
earned less after adjustments for inflation than in any year since 1961.
In the context of these real financial disappointments, it is not particularly surprising to discover that taxpayers increasingly resist supporting
welfare and other income-maintenance programs paid for by their
taxes.

But perhaps there is a deeper reason for this attitude: after all,
persistent poverty in a sense mocks our belief that we are a people in a
land of plenty, a land of opportunity. And, obviously, if this is such a

land of opportunity, we should be able to eradicate poverty. If we can't, then just as obviously something or someone must take the blame—and, unfortunately, those blamed are usually the victims—for our failure to achieve that goal. On a more practical level, these observations need to be sharpened by noting the personal and public strategies pursued for the last decade by many who live in the United States and their leaders.

With all our wealth, we have not been using our resources to ensure continued prosperity. Recent presidents have preferred coercive intervention to policies aimed at developing our human resources. While it heads the list of countries in per capita incarceration, the United States has fallen behind eighteen other countries in its rate of infant mortality. A larger proportion of our children grow up in poverty than do those in any other major industrial country. In a science test administered in the mid-1980s to fourteen-year-olds in thirteen countries, our children performed marginally better than those in Hong Kong and thereby captured twelfth place.

In spite of our economic power and the obvious need for domestic policy intervention, little is happening at any level of government, apart from painful adjustments to current cyclical economic problems. There is no more troubling national political problem than the current disenchantment with government and no greater challenge than to develop progressive programs within this constraint. The present welfare system stands as a reasonable proxy for all such disappointments with the lack of economic progress and the stultification of government programs. Setting aside the many attacks on the current system that depend on emotion and prejudice, serious students of what to do about welfare have focused on two major questions: first, do we need a new conception of what welfare is meant to accomplish and, second, is it possible to realize improvement in the system by reforming its management?

Richard P. Nathan examines both these issues in terms of new-style workfare, a set of programs that includes job training, education, child care, and other social services. Nathan believes that if properly designed and implemented this approach will help those on welfare to become self-sufficient. Workfare, as a concept, met considerable resistance when first put forward. But while it still generates controversy, the notion of viewing the welfare system as a means to move people into the mainstream—to make them full participants in society through programs providing support, encouragement, training, and participation—is receiving increasingly serious consideration.

Nathan's book contains a mixture of philosophy, case histories, and practical steps for managers to help the reader comprehend the world of welfare providers and recipients. Nathan is especially adept at explaining the internal workings of the welfare bureaucracy and the clash of differing, sincerely held beliefs about how to "solve" the dependency problem. He examines the evidence on why programs succeed or fail. While highly prescriptive and offering substantial proposals for reform, he does not minimize the sheer difficulty of reversing some patterns of poverty.

It is important to keep in mind that Nathan's book is more than a story about how hard it is to reform welfare. It is also a political science book about a neglected dimension of the United States governmental process—implementation policy. Nathan, a long-time observer of government, is the author of the widely read book *The Administrative Presidency,* which deals with the importance of implementation—what happens to policies after they are made—in the national government. This new book, *Turning Promises into Performance,* is the logical sequel to that volume. It concentrates on the way leaders of state agencies can serve as change agents and describes the pitfalls and barriers that make this no easy task. For many readers, the governance themes woven skillfully through this book will provide a valuable addition to the existing scholarship on U.S. domestic public affairs. Nathan, having served both in government and academe, has just the right blend of experience and scholarship to make the case—and he does so forcefully—that political leaders neglect the implementation dimension of the policy process at their peril.

Nathan is currently provost of the Nelson A. Rockefeller College of Public Affairs and Policy and director of the Rockefeller Institute of Government of the State University of New York at Albany. The Twentieth Century Fund supported his work as part of its ongoing commitment to social issues—a commitment expressed, for example, by earlier Fund works such as Charles Moskos's *Call to Civic Service* and Robert Haveman's *Starting Even.*

The Fund thanks Dick Nathan for his efforts. We believe that his work will help enliven and sharpen the continuing debate about how to provide effective relief and opportunity to our poorest citizens.

Richard C. Leone, President
The Twentieth Century Fund
September 1992

Preface

Although the field of social policy is filled with good intentions, those who formulate such policies tend to give short shrift to the business of carrying them out. New policies are often intended as agents of institutional change, representing efforts to change the signals and services of large organizations. They are only important if they penetrate the bureaucracy and change its behavior. Whether it is in education, health, welfare, or some other field, the process of converting good intentions into good results is the basis on which citizens judge—and appropriately so—the capacity of government. Those interested in public policy need to devote more time and attention to these institutional and implementation dimensions of the governmental process. After all, no matter how well-crafted the policy, how pure the intent, unless effective programs are put in place nothing will happen. The aim of this book is to help people learn how to get things done in government. My argument is that we need to make basic changes in the way we recruit, prepare, reward, and treat top managers in government so that good intentions by politicians become good results for citizens.

Many experts and government officials were generous with their time in providing information for this examination of the policy implementation process. I want to express appreciation to John Samples, my project officer at the Twentieth Century Fund, for his aid and encouragement and to Beverly Goldberg, the editorial director of the Fund. Martha Derthick, Erica Baum, and Rebecca Blank read and commented on drafts. Brenda Kilianski served ably as my research assistant. Carol Kuhl, Nan Nash, Laurie Norris, and Brenda Kilianski provided valuable assistance in the preparation of the manuscript.

I especially wish to thank many helpful respondents in the five case-study states—Arkansas, California, Massachusetts, Michigan, and New Jersey. I discussed this research with the governors of all but one of the five states (Michigan). President Bill Clinton, governor of Arkansas during the period of the field research for this book, played a major national role on welfare policy issues in the 1980s and provided strong leadership on behalf of the nation's governors in the enactment of the Family Support Act of 1988 described in chapter 3.

Appreciation is also expressed to the staff of the Manpower Demonstration Research Corporation and to Jan Hagen and Irene Lurie, who performed major studies that I relied upon heavily in writing this book. It should be noted that I serve as chair of the Board of the Manpower Demonstration Research Corporation and assisted Hagen and Lurie in their research. However, the ideas and interpretations of events and studies presented in this book are my responsibility alone.

My wife, Mary N. Nathan, who has been a strong and patient supporter in writing this book and others, shares with me the sense of excitement and fulfillment that such hard work provides.

Richard P. Nathan
Albany, New York

1

The Shadow Land

This book is about three things that are interconnected—*leadership, management, and behavior*—in state and local government in the United States. I argue that leaders in domestic government in the United States need to give greater attention to management and that the ultimate purpose is to affect the behavior of government agencies. American government expends a great deal of time and energy on what to do, but not nearly enough time and energy on how to do it. The American governmental process is skin deep. The domestic management challenge, however, involves vital organs. Penetration of state and local bureaucracies is necessary to institute new ideas. In the poem "The Hollow Men" T. S. Eliot wrote:

> Between the idea
> And the reality
> Between the motion
> And the act
> Falls the Shadow

This shadow land between policy and its execution is the subject of my exploration. The phrase makes one think of activity we do not know enough about, an area in which there is movement that is not well understood. I want to shine a light on this activity in order to understand it better myself. Even more than that, I would like to illuminate the field for others.

The case material I use to do this involves the implementation by state and local welfare agencies of what I call "new-style work-fare," a domestic policy in which I have personally had a long interest and close involvement. I hope this gives me an advantage in drawing out lessons about implementation in the illusive shadow land of our governmental process.

The term *workfare* has had a checkered history. In the seventies it was an anathema to liberals. However, the way the term came to be used in the eighties reflects a new meaning that is more acceptable to liberals highlighting the provision of job training and social services for welfare families in order to enable the family head to enter the labor force and ultimately become self-sufficient. New-style workfare embodies a political bargain between liberals and conservatives. The operative concept is *mutual obligation,* which combines an obligation on the part of the state to provide services and on the part of recipients to participate in these services. In the interest of truth in labeling, I should make it clear that this approach to welfare reform is one that I favor. However, the purpose of this book is not to urge others to accept my views on welfare. It is a book about government. It focuses not so much on the substance of new-style workfare as on its implementation.

Several chapters in this book describe the welfare-employment programs of five states—Arkansas, California, Massachusetts, Michigan, and New Jersey. Massachusetts was the flagship state in setting up a new work-welfare program in 1983 under Governor Michael S. Dukakis. The other four case-study states adopted new-style workfare programs in the mid-eighties emphasizing training, job placement, education, and child care services.

The sample states, along with others, operated their new-style workfare programs under amendments to President Reagan's first budget act passed in 1981. The 1981 Budget Act authorized the states to set up demonstration programs to prepare welfare family heads for work and facilitate their entering the job market. Seven years later President Reagan signed the Family Support Act of 1988 that extended this authority, making it nationwide. By then all states could build on a considerable base of experience to achieve the purposes of the new law. In institutional terms the aim of both of these laws (the 1981 Budget Act and the 1988 Family Support Act) is to transform state welfare agencies from being primarily welfare payment systems into *service* systems that highlight job preparation and child care for welfare families. Did this transformation happen? What is involved in trying to put these kinds of new policies into effect?

I turn next to an anecdote that pulls together several of the major ideas in the chapters that follow. On February 3, 1992, New York's senior senator, Daniel Patrick Moynihan, held a hearing on what for him is a familiar subject—welfare policy. The focus was on a law just enacted in New Jersey. The law, like many others in the field, combines carrots and sticks to try to change the behavior of welfare family heads, predominantly single women with children, so they can ultimately stop receiving welfare and become self-sufficient.

The Moynihan hearing in February 1992 came at a time when welfare policy in the nation was becoming more conservative and focusing on efforts to save money and restrict benefits. Rising welfare roles and frustration with government in general were reflected in this backlash toward welfare; many states were cutting benefits and imposing new requirements on welfare families. The New Jersey law included a provision stating that if a woman conceived a child while on welfare there would be no welfare benefit (an extra sixty-four dollars per month) for that child. The aim of this provision was to influence the behavior of parents, to discourage them from conceiving a child out of wedlock in situations where they did not have the resources to raise the child. In many cases like these, laws are meant not so much to influence the poor as to send a signal to well-off voters. The sixty-four-dollar question was, Is this a good idea?

At the Moynihan hearing a panel of six experts (this author among them) discussed the new state restrictions on welfare, referring to them as a "new paternalism." The irony of the new paternalism is that it came on top of the Family Support Act of 1988, passed just four years earlier, of which Moynihan had been a chief author. The Family Support Act of 1988 emphasizes work, school, self-support, and family responsibility under the new welfare reform program and was heralded by President Reagan when he signed the act as the most important advance in welfare policy in fifty years. The more I listened to the panel discussion, the more I was struck by one point:

The new paternalism was trying to influence the wrong behavior.

Welfare mothers do not spend their day reading congressional hearing records, listening to C-SPAN, or following accounts of debates on social policy in the *New York Times* or the *Washington Post*. If we are serious about influencing their behavior, we need an instrument. And the main instrument is the state and local bureaucracies that administer welfare programs. It is their behavior we need to change, and we already had a law on the books to do so in 1988—the Family Support Act of 1988. Yet before the 1988 law was given a real chance, new efforts were being made to turn the welfare world upside down by enacting another set of bold and broad reforms catering more to the anger of taxpayers than anything else.

Let me now go back to the three interconnected themes of this book—*leadership, management,* and *behavior.* I am interested in the kinds of leadership needed to manage public agencies in ways that change their behavior to achieve new policy goals. In essence the 1981 and 1988 welfare reform laws presented us with an implementation challenge. Political leaders sought, or at least talked about, having state and local welfare bureaucracies operate in ways that changed the signals and services of huge public welfare bureaucracies, each with their own histories, values, and structures. Yet making government policies and carrying them out are two different worlds. Let me explain what I mean.

We are blessed in America with a lively, competitive (one could say, hyperactive) form of political pluralism. Access to government is widespread. Ideas rub up against each other in hot debates about public purposes—the hottest ones often being about matters close to home in fields such as education, health, criminal justice, and the treatment of the poor. Unfortunately, leaders in government are often so busy jockeying for position to put their names and fingerprints on new policies that they have little time and energy to devote to carrying out "old" policies, even if those policies are just a few months old. Management is complicated and boring. It is also very difficult. You have to wrestle with unions, the civil service, purchasing, contracting, and financial rules, and myriad other administrative matters. Perhaps because of this, new policies, like new cars, become forgotten used policies very fast.

Another experience I had in New Jersey, this one going back to 1988, serves to convey the spirit of this new political bargain of welfare policy. Under Governor Thomas H. Kean, the state of New Jersey in 1986 instituted pilot programs in two cities (Newark and Camden) for teenage female welfare family heads. I visited the pilot site in Newark early in 1988. I was picked up at the train station by James Walsh, a case manager for the new program. Caught in traffic on the way to the site, Walsh told me his story. He had previously been a social-work specialist with the state government and had just been recruited to be a case manager for the "Teen Progress" demonstration in Newark. Walsh's caseload included girls aged thirteen to nineteen. At the time, they received $322 per month in welfare benefits under the federally aided Aid for Families with Dependent Children program (AFDC). Under the pilot project teenagers referred by the Essex County welfare agency (Newark is in Essex County) were required to participate in a range of activities, including orientation, testing, education, training, parenting classes, and counseling. The aim was to get the participants to finish their education and learn how to manage their affairs and raise their children so they would not always be on welfare. Day care was provided for their children while the mothers went to school or partic-ipated in other activities. If a teenager referred to the program failed to participate, she was supposed to be penalized. She lost half of her AFDC benefit, the mother's portion of the payment.

I asked the case worker, James Walsh, what he thought about taking money away from welfare families under this sanctioning procedure. He said that originally he did not like it and resisted doing it. How-ever, by the time of our conversation, he had changed his mind. He had sanctioned five of "his girls," one of whom had subsequently returned to the program. "They test you," he said, "to see if you'll sanction." He decided that sanctioning was necessary to indicate the seriousness of the new policy highlighting education and employment preparation. Walsh put a sign up in his office:

NO MORE MISTER NICE GUY!

James Walsh had become a carrier of the new policy. He seemed to believe in it. However, a close look at the setting of the Newark Teen Progress demonstration shows that James Walsh and his associates were swimming against the tide in Essex County. (County govern-ments in New Jersey administer welfare programs, including the AFDC program, under state supervision.) The county welfare bureaucracy was described by Walsh's supervisor, Yvonne Johnston, as "hidebound" and strongly opposed to the new concept. Johnston, a former AFDC recipient, was also a carrier of the new policy; she was a defender of the philosophy of the Teen Progress program. "This is not just a paper program," she said, "I can get what I need. We say to participants: 'You are an adult.'" Johnston said the ideas of the new approach were hardest to get across to county welfare workers. She complained about the negative attitude and resistance of the Essex County welfare department. Johnston said she was proud of her staff and specifically of Walsh's "No More Mister Nice Guy" stance.

The implementation challenge of this program gets us back to my question, *Whose behavior do we care about?* Under new-style workfare, as under New Jersey's Teen Progress program, it is not enough to pass laws and issue regulations requiring poor people to behave in certain ways. Leadership and management are needed to influence the behavior of the bureaucracy.

Two characteristics of the new-style workfare programs of the eighties make them especially interesting as case material for studying policy implementation. One is their breadth. They involve a wide array of organizations—welfare agencies, child care providers, employment services, training programs, schools and community colleges, as well as health and transportation agencies. This can be thought of as the horizontal/coordination challenge of welfare employment strategies.

A second characteristic of welfare employment strategies that makes them good case material for the study of policy implementation is their vertical or federalism dimension. They involve the national government, state governments, county governments, other local governments (for example, school districts), and thousands of community organizations that administer services for welfare families. Studying these programs reveals a great deal about the nature and workings of American government.

Implementation is hard to assess because we lack good measurement tools. There is no Richter scale that measures how much the earth moves when a new policy is adopted. This may explain why the subject gets short shrift not only from political leaders but also from social scientists. Nonetheless I am determined to press the argument that two communities—both the governmental and the research communities— should give more attention to the implementation dimension of the American governmental process.

Henry James is said to have confided to a young writer that the key to a novel is to have a theme that runs through it like an iron rod. The iron-rod theme of this book is that we need to give more attention to policy implementation. My test case is whether the policy bargain of new-style workfare struck in Washington and state capitals can be kept in local welfare offices. I am especially interested in the role of the managers of state agencies and the ways in which they can motivate others and advance goals such as those of new-style workfare. The challenge for leaders who seek to play this role is a formidable one.

2

The Origins of "New-Style Workfare"

The nomenclature of the welfare field tells us a great deal about issues that have arisen over the years. The term *workfare* is especially interesting. It came into use nationally in the early seventies in the debate over President Richard M. Nixon's proposals for welfare reform.

NIXON'S FAMILY ASSISTANCE PLAN

To the surprise of many observers, Nixon decided in his first year in office to advance a bold (one could even say, radical) welfare reform plan. At the time AFDC caseloads and costs were rising rapidly, as was the visibility of the program as a political issue. The number of people on AFDC almost doubled between 1961 when 3.5 million received AFDC payments and 1969, the year Nixon was inaugurated, when the total on AFDC was 6.7 million. The costs of the AFDC program more than doubled in this period. Something had to be done.[1]

Up to this time two basic approaches competed for attention in welfare policy-making. In the simplest terms, the choice reflects the old adage of the difference between giving people a fish (the so-called "income strategy" in welfare parlance) and teaching them to fish (the "service strategy"). Nixon's welfare reform plan, unveiled in August 1969, was supposed to encompass both strategies. However, the main and newest feature of his Family Assistance Plan (FAP) involved the income strategy. I refer to Nixon's plan for the establishment of what many commentators at the time referred to as a "guaranteed income" both for poor families headed by one person and for two-parent or intact poor families. This approach to welfare reform, also called the "negative income tax" approach, was championed by economists in the seventies. The basic aim was to strengthen work incentives by allowing poor family heads who work to keep more of their earned income than they would have been able to retain under AFDC.

Referring to the relationship between benefits and earnings, critics have complained that the AFDC "tax rate" was too high. To take a hypothetical example, if a single parent in a female-headed poor family, who is entitled to a $400 per month AFDC payment, goes to work and earns $400 and loses her AFDC benefit dollar-for-dollar, this is referred to as a *100 percent tax* on her earnings: each dollar of additional earnings causes her to lose a dollar of welfare benefits.

Although AFDC does not actually work this way, and did not in 1969 when Nixon came to office, there was widespread and legitimate concern that the welfare tax rate (also called the benefit-reduction rate) was too high in many states and that welfare family heads had little or no incentive to work. Other factors, such as the loss of health benefits under Medicaid if a woman heading a welfare family went to work, the hassle involved in arranging child care, and getting to and keeping a low-wage job, were seen as additional work disincentives. Reformers favoring the negative income tax approach—the income strategy— argued that the welfare benefit-reduction rate had to be reduced. They said it should be not higher than 50 percent—that is, allowing a welfare family head to keep fifty cents in welfare benefits for each additional dollar in earnings.

Government economists had urged Lyndon Johnson to embrace this income-strategy approach to welfare reform as part of his famous war on poverty. They wanted him to cover all poor families under what they said would be a much fairer and more equitable system than AFDC. They criticized AFDC for only covering single-parent families and discriminating against the working poor—intact families with incomes lower than welfare or low enough to qualify to be on welfare.

These experts in government in the Johnson years urged that AFDC be abolished and replaced with a new system that treated all poor families the same and encouraged them to be self-supporting and eventually to get off welfare. President Johnson, however, was not buying. He and his chief adviser, Wilbur Cohen, who was secretary of Health, Education, and Welfare (HEW), turned a deaf ear to these experts within the government who were advocating this approach to fighting poverty. Johnson's war on poverty took a very different tack.

Among the insiders in government advocating the idea of a negative income tax was economist Worth Bateman, a deputy assistant secretary of HEW, who continued to serve at the beginning of the Nixon administration. As it turned out, Bateman was influential in the decisions made concerning the welfare reform plan announced by President Nixon in 1969. In an HEW departmental planning memo written just prior to Nixon's inauguration, Bateman urged "as a long-term goal of the department the development of a comprehensive income maintenance program which keeps those who can't work out of poverty and supplements the earnings of those who do work without destroying incentives." [2] Bateman added: "This goal implies substantially broader coverage than is provided under our present programs." [3] Advocating this negative income tax approach would certainly be a long shot now that the Republicans were coming into office. Surprisingly, however, this policy was adopted by Nixon.

The battle for the president's soul on this issue within the Nixon administration is the most interesting domestic policy episode of his tenure. The ubiquitous and always influential social policy expert, Daniel Patrick Moynihan, headed the Urban Affairs Council in the Nixon White House in 1969. He quickly became a particular favorite of the new president. He also became an early advocate of the negative income tax idea as put forward by Bateman and his colleagues at HEW. In his retrospective book on these events, Moynihan tells about the rejection of the guaranteed income idea under President Johnson, cites Bateman's work approvingly, and says, "It is perhaps the ultimate irony that the Nixon proposal for a negative income tax was drafted by Democratic advocates who not months earlier had the same proposal rejected by the Johnson administration." [4]

Among Nixon appointees, the principal opponent of the negative income tax idea was Martin Anderson, an assistant in the White House working under Arthur Burns. Burns was a senior adviser on domestic policy and "counselor" to the president. He had been chairman of the

Council of Economic Advisers under Eisenhower when Nixon was vice president and was personally close to Nixon. A pipe-sucking conservative, something of a curmudgeon, who talked slowly and knew his way around Washington, Burns was appalled that Nixon was even tempted by the negative income tax idea.

Like Moynihan, Martin Anderson, Burns's aide, has written a retrospective book about this period; unlike Moynihan's book, however, Anderson's book stoutly opposes the idea of the negative income tax. In a passage that captures the tensions of the period, Anderson says, "The principle of a guaranteed income, buried in the original FAP proposal, soon became the crucial point of contention between the advocates of FAP, led by Moynihan, and the opponents of FAP, led by the counselor to the President, Arthur Burns." [5] Burns and Anderson failed to win the day against FAP, but succeeded in getting a statement included in Nixon's 1969 speech announcing his new welfare reform plan that thoroughly muddied the waters. In it, Nixon insisted that the new plan was not a guaranteed income:

> This national floor under income for working or dependent families is not a "guaranteed income." Under the guaranteed income proposal, everyone would be assured a minimum income, regardless of how much he was capable of earning, regardless of what his need was, regardless of whether or not he was willing to work.
>
> During the presidential campaign last year, I opposed such a plan. I oppose it now and I will continue to oppose it, for this reason: a guaranteed income would undermine the incentive to work; the family assistance plan that I propose increases the incentive to work.[6]

For Anderson, and probably also for Nixon, the argument that FAP was not a guaranteed income was based on its employment provisions. Nixon's FAP covered all poor families in the same system, sought to lower the welfare benefit-reduction rate, raised family welfare benefits in many states, and broadened their coverage. At the same time, it contained what was supposed to be a strong work requirement and strong work-facilitation features. The plan required all single-parent welfare family heads with children over six years of age to work. It placed the same requirement on at least one family member in intact welfare families regardless of the age of the children. Nixon's plan also provided money for employment and training services to enable welfare family heads to obtain preparation for work. In situations in which not enough jobs existed, it provided money for public service jobs. Despite Nixon's insistence that this hybrid was not a guaranteed income, that welfare family heads *had* to work, all of the congressional debate and most of the news coverage of FAP focused on the effect of the income support payments for all eligible poor families.

THE FAP DEBATE

This debate over the meaning and purpose of FAP brings my issue of implementation front and center. Richard Nixon and others believed that the work requirement and job service and facilitation features of FAP would be implemented. They were not window dressing. As a result, able-bodied adults in welfare families would go to work; they would not receive welfare payments unless they were getting ready to work. Skeptics on the conservative side did not accept this crucial implementation assumption. They believed that the work requirement and employment services of FAP would not be put into effect as planned. As a result, a major effect of Nixon's more comprehensive assured-payment plan would "expose" more people to the welfare system. In so doing, its conservative critics said FAP would undermine, rather than enhance, the incentive for able-bodied welfare family heads to take and retain jobs. This is the essence of the debate between liberals and conservatives on the idea of a negative income tax.

As it turned out, some features of Nixon's welfare reform plan (the work requirements and his proposal for a national minimum benefit for the poor who are aged and disabled) were enacted into law.[7] But the most radical part of Nixon's proposal, the comprehensive national minimum benefit for welfare families, was not.[8] Liberals would claim— some did—that it was an idea ahead of its time.

The decision process for Nixon's welfare reform plan at the highest levels of his administration reveals the way many politicians have fudged this basic issue of the relationship between the income and the employment roads to welfare reform. These politicians—including Richard Nixon and Jimmy Carter—have tried to travel both roads at once. They sought, and still seek, both to require and facilitate work and at the same time to give more aid on a broader basis. The essential dilemma is that the objectives of the service or employment strategy of requiring and facilitating work in the complex environment in which poor family heads (mostly females) live involve hugely difficult implementation tasks. If these objectives of the Nixon and Carter hybrid plans did not work, then their main effect would be increased welfare benefits and caseloads. Although this is a simplification, it is the way I believe this debate should be viewed and brings me back to my theme: *much depended on the implementation of the service components of both the Nixon and Carter welfare reform plans.* Previous efforts to do this—to provide training and job services to get people off welfare—had come up short of the mark.

As a nation, we have frequently saluted the work ethic, but the troops have failed to march. People such as those mentioned earlier who work for the Essex County, New Jersey, welfare department have immense influence on the behavior of the poor. They frequently have their own ideas about how the poor should be treated. Their philosophy stresses compassion and highlights the barriers poor family heads face in the labor market. They resist the idea of a work requirement and the work-facilitation features that politicians blithely adopt in laws that, as I have noted earlier, are often aimed more at satisfying the rich than helping the poor among us. Yet, unless welfare workers at the ground level behave so that the job preparation and facilitation systems really work, the provision of higher and broader welfare benefits to welfare family heads, made in order to increase work incentives, can backfire.

This is a complicated subject, but the basic point is simple: if a decision is made to lower the welfare benefit-reduction rate then it is possible that there will be more people on welfare because it takes longer (that is, goes further up the income scale) for the welfare benefit to be reduced to zero, at what is known in the trade as the "break-even point." If this happens, if there are more people on the welfare rolls because of the higher break-even point, one view holds that there will be more "exposure" to welfare. Conservatives do not like to expose people to welfare. They argue that exposing additional people to welfare may lure or trap them into dependency. Nixon's answer was, No, the people are required to work, and we have training and placement services to help them do so. But if down in Essex County welfare caseworkers do not march, if they do not enforce the work requirement and provide the needed job services, his answer will not wash.

To sum up, conservative critics of Nixon's Family Assistance Plan did not believe the work requirement or job services he proposed would offset the case-enlargement effects of his plan. Its net result, they felt, would be to put more people on welfare and increase welfare spending. This conundrum of welfare policy has tripped up many well-intentioned politicians, and even welfare experts, and has been the source of a tremendous amount of confusion, even mischief, in social policy.

LET'S CALL IT "WORKFARE"

Language, as I said at the beginning of this chapter, is important in viewing political history. The August 1969 television speech to the nation in which Nixon announced his domestic program, his "New Federalism," contained this paragraph: "In the final analysis, we cannot talk our way out of poverty; we cannot legislate our way out of poverty, but this Nation can work its way out of poverty. What America needs now is not more welfare, but more 'workfare.' "[9]

The speech writer was William Safire. The word *workfare* was put in quotation marks. Safire hoped it would catch on as the name for Nixon's whole new welfare reform plan. It did not. But the word has gotten around anyway. Twenty years later, when Safire wrote about his experience working on Nixon's 1969 national television address on his domestic agenda, he claimed credit—which he deserves—for putting forward the term *workfare* to describe Nixon's welfare reform plan. In 1988 Safire said that the word *workfare* is now widely used to describe welfare employment programs and is "rolling merrily along," even though the *Oxford English Dictionary* had given someone else (Charles Evers of Mississippi) credit for coining this term: "That's all right; I may not have been the first to use the word, but I had a hand in its nationwide launch and feel a stepfather's pride." [10]

Although *workfare* did not catch on as the name for Nixon's welfare plan, it did come into public use in the debate over the plan. As I reconstruct this history, *workfare* came into its widest usage three years later, in 1972, as the name the press attached to the "work-for-your-welfare" or work-relief approach to welfare. Credit for this word-smithing goes to former U.S. Senator Russell B. Long (Democrat from Louisiana) who was chairman of the Senate Finance Committee when Nixon's FAP plan was being considered by that body. Unfortunately for Nixon, Senator Long was dead set against the negative income tax idea and fought Nixon's FAP proposal. He was ably joined by the ranking minority member of the Senate Finance Committee, John J. Williams of Delaware. Russell Long advanced his own welfare reform plan, which sought to restrict welfare aid to able-bodied adults as payment for work. Private and nonprofit employers would receive a 50 percent wage subsidy for up to six months for hiring welfare family heads.

Long's alternative to FAP was not enacted in the seventies, although it was enacted as one option states could adopt in the 1981 Budget Act. Because these subsidy funds, in effect, are "diverted" from welfare benefits to wages, such plans are referred to as "grant diversion" programs. Even though it was not adopted in the seventies, Long's proposal played an important role in the defeat of the family-payment portion of the Nixon plan. In the press, Long's alternative to FAP was referred to as "workfare." It was portrayed in a pejorative way by liberals who criticized Long's approach as "slavefare." Perhaps Safire should have called Nixon's version "workfair" (spelled differently) as a way of characterizing this delicate ideological balancing act and distinguishing this term from the work-relief idea.

To finish up on the semantics, *workfare* in the 1970s was seen as a restrictive and punitive approach to welfare reform, as a term connoting welfare payments in the form of compensation for work only. *New-style workfare,* as the term came to be used in the 1980s, is broader and less harsh. It refers to a range of strategies that link welfare payments with services intended to prepare able-bodied family heads on welfare for work and to facilitate their entry into the labor force.

This shift involves more than words. As stated earlier, a truce appeared to have been worked out between liberals and conservatives in the eighties involving an agreement on aid for able-bodied, working-age poor adults with children. The focus was not on benefits, as was the case in the seventies, but rather on the service side. In this sense, the strategy on welfare shifted from being an income strategy in the seventies to being a service strategy in the eighties. Rather than giving poor people fish, the main push in the eighties was on teaching them *how to fish*.

But we are still on a slippery slope. Would welfare recipients respond to the carrots and sticks of "new-style workfare"? What about implementation? Would the troops march? Would state and local governments, agency heads, and welfare agency personnel salute the new policy and try to put it into effect? As I have already explained, the new policy came in two bites: first, the demonstration authority—that is, permission to test this approach—which was included in the 1981

Budget Act; and second, the Family Support Act of 1988 that made this approach nationwide. We turn next to look more closely at the way new-style workfare was viewed by Ronald Reagan, beginning with his role as governor in California and including his role in the enactment of the 1981 Budget Act and the Family Support Act of 1988.

CHAPTER

3

Changes Under Reagan

The dream of many politicians when it comes to welfare has been to make it self-destruct. Writing in 1971, Gilbert Y. Steiner, an authority on the history of welfare programs, said, "Welfare is a public business whose liquidation under honorable conditions has been a stated goal of political leaders from Franklin Roosevelt to Richard Nixon."[1] Steiner quotes a letter written by Roosevelt in 1934: "I cannot say so out loud but I hope to be able to substitute work for relief."[2]

Laws to emphasize work and job preparation for welfare family heads were also favored by FDR's successors. Such changes were enacted in 1962 under President Kennedy. Five years later, in 1967, further provisions were adopted under President Johnson to strengthen the bond between work and welfare. And, as I have already noted, the connection between work and welfare was front and center on President Nixon's agenda. Although all of these presidents—Roosevelt, Kennedy, Johnson, and Nixon—are associated with the idea of substituting work for welfare, there is no modern president who is more staunchly in this prowork camp than Ronald Reagan.

REAGAN AS GOVERNOR

In his first campaign for governor of California in 1967, Reagan railed against runaway welfare costs. As it turned out, however, he took little concrete action to reform California's welfare program during his first term as governor.[3] In this period, the AFDC caseload in California more than doubled, going from 769,000 to 1,566,000, a trend that was also occurring nationally. According to Fred Doolittle, "If Ronald Reagan had not won reelection in 1970 and returned to fight the welfare monster another day, he would be remembered as the governor who unwittingly presided over the largest increase in the AFDC caseload in the history of California or any other state."[4] But Reagan came back to the battle another day, making welfare reform a major issue of his gubernatorial reelection campaign in 1970 and the first priority of his second term.

Once reelected, Reagan moved quickly. His biographer, Lou Cannon, believes Reagan's role on welfare in the early seventies—both nationally, opposing Nixon's FAP plan and offering his own alternative national plan, and at the state level—marks the point at which he "came of age politically."[5] Reagan and his welfare director, Robert B. Carleson, fought for welfare changes on many fronts—in the courts, in the legislature, and in Washington. Reagan's slogan was "to aid the needy and not the greedy." Three purposes were highlighted: cutting off working recipients, increasing family responsibility, and stopping welfare fraud.

Reagan announced his California welfare reform plan in January 1971. He submitted legislation in March of that year, which won quick enactment. In April 1971 he met with President Nixon to start negotiations on the waivers of federal law needed to set up his reform program. According to Doolittle: "When Reagan is able to talk about what he wants to talk about, few can compete with his powers of persuasion. Reagan's reelection provided political momentum that allowed him to define the questions for the welfare reform debate. Though Democrats controlled the legislature they did not have the two-thirds majority needed to pass budget appropriations or override the governor's veto, so Reagan's reelection meant he was in the driver's seat."[6]

Reagan's 1971 California welfare reform plan required adult recipients to work off their welfare checks in community public-service jobs if regular employment was not available in either the public or private sectors. The plan was called CWEP, for the community work experience program, and the idea, with its specific designation CWEP, was carried over and included in Reagan's presidential policies.

CWEP assignments are ordinarily time-limited (six months or a year). They are supposed to provide useful work experience and training that will eventually help participants find their way into the regular labor force. An additional objective is the provision of service to the community—for example, building maintenance, park and street clean-up, school corridor monitors, and clerical support for police, fire, libraries, social services, parks, recreation, and other public agencies. Typically, under CWEP, the hours of participation are equal to the recipient's welfare benefit divided by the minimum wage.

The consensus among welfare experts is that Reagan's 1971 California reforms were unsuccessful. Although California's welfare rolls declined during Reagan's governorship, two-thirds of the people on AFDC saw their benefits rise. Moreover, the number of people who participated in the community work experience program was very small. Analysts claim the rolls in California would have declined anyway after 1970. Doolittle says, "CWEP looks as if it was intended to be all mirrors and no real substance." [7] But to Reagan, his California welfare reforms of 1971 were a great victory, one that became a central theme of his presidential campaigns in 1976 and 1980. In 1976 he claimed, "When I took office, California was the welfare capital of the nation. The caseload was increasing 40,000 a month. We turned that 40,000 a month increase into an 8,000 a month decrease. We returned to the taxpayers $2 billion and we increased grants to the truly needy by forty-three percent." [8]

REAGAN AS PRESIDENT

In 1981, ten years after the enactment of the California Welfare Reform Act, Ronald Reagan, as president of the United States, continued to press for work-oriented welfare reforms. Unlike Nixon, his focus was on the state level and included a community work experience program, which became a source of controversy, although not hot controversy. Writing in 1983, Leonard Goodwin says he believes such "make-work activities" had become "a way of spending administrative funds to harass heads of households who cannot find jobs that allow them to support their families." [9] In Goodwin's opinion, such work-for-your-welfare arrangements reduced "expectations of achieving economic independence." Goodwin says work experience programs provide "the American public with the illusion that something is being done about the welfare problem when, in fact, nothing positive is being accomplished." [10] Over the years, liberal welfare experts and advocates have criticized the mandatory (and in their view punitive) character of work programs such as CWEP for welfare family heads. As I have said before, the meaning of "workfare" in the seventies referred narrowly and usually pejoratively to these and similar required-work and work-relief approaches to aiding poor adults. This category included both single people, aided under what in most states is called "general assistance" programs, and able-bodied adult family heads under AFDC, (mostly, of course, women).

On the other side, conservative critics did not think these schemes went far enough. In *The New Republic* in July 1986, journalist Mickey Kaus said: "Welfare doesn't work. Work 'incentives' don't work. Training doesn't work. Work 'requirements' don't work. 'Work experience' doesn't work and even workfare doesn't quite work. Only work works." [11] Mickey Kaus and other conservative welfare critics pressed for radical change going beyond Reagan's CWEP approach. There are few hard-liners as hard as Kaus, who also stated: "The short, nasty answer is that if a mother turns down the state's offer of a job with which she might support her children, and as a result her children live in squalor and filth, then she has neglected a basic task of parenthood. She is subject to the laws that already provide for removal of a child from an unfit home." [12]

Kaus drew a distinction between "hard workfare" (his preferred solution) and "soft workfare," which he called "whistle-while-you-workfare." The latter, he says, emphasized "the positive things working can do for a recipient, in which work requirements are not really applied to people who resist them." Kaus identified me (my views have already been stated) as an advocate of "soft workfare." [13]

Some experts, such as Lawrence Mead, tried to find a middle ground. Mead was critical of "the permissive character" of federal government programs for the poor, which in his view, "have as yet no serious requirements that employable recipients work in return for support." [14]

> Because of the way social policy is approached in Washington, as well as for electoral and constitutional reasons, federal politicians tend to use social programs simply to give deserving people good things, seldom to set standards for how they ought to behave. Thus, dependent groups are shielded from the pressures to function well that impinge on other Americans. [15]

All these ideas swirled around in debates about welfare in the early eighties when Ronald Reagan entered the White House. However, at the beginning of his presidency, it did not appear that welfare reform would be a high priority. No signal was given by the new president that welfare reform would be an early top priority.

THE 1981 BUDGET ACT

Early in 1981, under the leadership of Reagan's dynamic budget director, David Stockman, the Reagan administration was preoccupied with the federal budget. The fiscal year 1982 budget had been submitted by Jimmy Carter in the interregnum period between the election and Reagan's inauguration. Reagan then revised the Carter plan in very active ways that reflected his own priorities. He increased defense spending substantially and proposed commensurate (in fact even bigger) reductions in domestic spending. As it turned out, and despite the fact that it was not planned this way, Reagan's budget revisions included changes in welfare.

What happened was interesting. During the transition between the presidential election and Inauguration Day, a team of advisers headed by Reagan aide Robert Carleson developed a welfare reform plan for Reagan. The plan was reviewed with the president-elect at a meeting at Blair House, the presidential guest house across the street from the White House.[16] In principle, Reagan approved the plan, which had goals similar to his California welfare reforms. It sought to remove working poor people from the welfare rolls and institute CWEP as an alternative to welfare. At that time, however, no decision was made as to when the welfare plan devised by the Carleson group would be unveiled.

In the meantime, the administration issued its first statement on its budget priorities in February 1981 to amend to Carter's 1982 budget. But there was a glitch. On close examination, the arithmetic of Stockman's plan turned out to be faulty. A shortfall of $3 billion was discovered just after Reagan's proposed revisions were announced. In the midst of this process, Carleson, now a White House special assistant to the president for policy development, had an inspiration. Why not simply insert the welfare reform plan, which projected savings roughly in line with the budget gap that needed to be plugged?

The moment was right and the numbers worked. Reagan's welfare reforms became part of his budget proposals. They included community work experience (CWEP) as one of the keys to Reagan's 1981 welfare plan. An April 1981 statement on the president's budget revisions stated:

> Each state shall be required to establish and maintain a community work experience program approved by the Secretary of Health and Human Services for those individuals required to work (exceptions would be the disabled, persons under 18 or over 65, those with very young children) as a condition of receiving AFDC. Community jobs would be provided if private sector jobs were unavailable. This mandatory requirement for AFDC recipients would encourage attachment to the labor force and self-support and would reduce the public assistance rolls so that more resources would be available for the truly needy.[17]

Reagan's approach was for a national CWEP program, *mandated for all states,* despite the limited results obtained a decade earlier in California. If an AFDC family head could not be placed in a regular private- or public-sector job, it was up to the community to provide a job. Testifying before Congress, Secretary Richard Schweiker of Health and Human Services said, "We believe that everyone receiving assistance who is capable of working should be involved in a work program." [18] Schweiker went on to say:

> These community work programs will increase the employability of recipients through actual work experience and training. They will encourage recipient identification with the labor market, provide recipients with a work history and develop the disciplines necessary for accepting employment in the regular economy. . . . They will eliminate current abuses in the program and, more importantly, lessen the burden of providing public assistance to those in need.[19]

The Reagan welfare reform plan as presented at this time had other major purposes in addition to CWEP. One was to change the structure of benefits to focus AFDC payments on the truly needy by diluting the work-incentive features that had been added to the AFDC program in 1967. These features allowed AFDC family heads to retain thirty dollars per month plus one-third of their earnings when they went to work. Their effect, as discussed in chapter 2, was to enable people to stay on the rolls longer when they went to work. Reagan eliminated this "$30 plus one-third" work-incentive provision in his 1981 budget amendments as a way of concentrating aid on the most needy and limiting welfare for the working poor.[20]

Although this strategy of "striking while the iron is hot" moved welfare quickly in the legislative process, important changes were made by Congress to water down Reagan's proposals. The most important change involved CWEP. Congress would not go along with requiring a community-service job program on a statewide basis in all states as Reagan had proposed. Instead, Congress (specifically the Senate Finance Committee) would only agree to provide authority for the states to *"experiment"* with CWEP, along with other approaches (including job search and training) aimed at enabling AFDC family heads to enter the labor force. Even for these demonstration programs, the Senate Finance Committee added language "to insure that job placement will have priority over participation in the community work experience program." [21] All in all, the debate on these provisions was low-key. A congressional history of this legislation notes that "[t]here was very little public debate on the CWEP legislation during the consideration by the Congress of the FY 1982 budget proposals." [22]

The 1981 Budget Act contained other welfare changes added by Congress. One was a provision coauthored by Senators Daniel Patrick Moynihan (Democrat, New York) and David Boren (Democrat, Oklahoma) that amended the work incentive program (called the WIN program) adopted in 1967. This program provided authority for state training and employment-service programs to prepare AFDC recipients for work and facilitate their entry into the labor force. The Moynihan-Boren amendment permitted the states to transfer the authority for administering WIN from the joint management of state employment and welfare agencies to a single state agency, which in most cases was the welfare agency. Although this may seem like a minor and technical change, it made an important difference in many states. Because relationships between state employment services and the welfare agency have been tense and strained in many states, to say the least, the authority to shift the responsibility for administering the WIN program to the welfare agency provided opportunities for reducing tensions and achieving management change.

The 1981 Budget Act allowed the states to require AFDC family heads to participate in either or both job search and CWEP; the states were given a choice of experimenting with job search alone or job search combined with CWEP. States were required to provide participants in such work-welfare programs with day care, transportation, and related services.

The 1981 Budget Act also gave the states authority to use money for AFDC payments to subsidize on-the-job training with private employers. As discussed in chapter 2, this is called "grant diversion." Under this authority the welfare recipient is paid a standard wage by the employer (i.e., standard for that employer and job), but part of the wage (usually half) is offset by having the government provide a time-limited wage subsidy to the employer. Although castigated by liberals in the seventies, the inclusion of this provision as one of the options available to the states in 1981 received relatively little notice.

Altogether, the work-welfare provisions of the 1981 Budget Act constituted a pretty rich menu of options for new programs (for which federal aid was available) that the states could use as ways to move people off welfare. True to Reagan's basic philosophy, the initiative rested with the states. As later chapters show, many states picked up on this new authority to experiment with what in this book I call "new-style workfare," a politically balanced combination of a stick in the form of the work requirement (one often not brandished with much seriousness) and a carrot in the form of services to help prepare welfare family heads for the labor force and facilitate their entry into regular jobs. During Reagan's presidency, there were many well-publicized efforts by the states to use this authority to reform their welfare systems. Although it was not a front-burner action area under Reagan, there was a lot going on, and "new-style workfare" was often seen in a positive light.

THE FAMILY SUPPORT ACT OF 1988

Having tasted victory in the welfare legislative arena in 1981, four years later, in 1985, when Reagan was reelected and his popularity was at a high point, the administration's top officials for domestic policy decided they should go to the well again for work-oriented welfare changes. In his 1986 State of the Union message, Reagan called upon Congress to work with his administration to enact welfare legislation "to escape the spider's web of dependency." Reagan quoted Franklin Roosevelt, "Welfare is a narcotic, a subtle destroyer of the human spirit." [23] He charged the White House Domestic Policy Council to present by December 1, 1986, "an evaluation of programs and a strategy for immediate action to meet the financial, educational, social, and safety concerns of poor families." [24] The president said: "I'm talking about real and lasting emancipation, because the success of welfare should be judged by how many of its recipients become independent of welfare." [25]

As I have shown, it is not unusual for political leaders to be talking about bold new policy changes in periods when action is under way, often in earnest and important ways, to change things under previously enacted policies long since forgotten. Now, Reagan was back at it. Only this time he apparently intended a more basic and far-reaching legislative overhaul of the current law.

However, even though the president was urging that this issue be on the agenda, prospects soon dimmed for major welfare legislation. The administration's standing was tarnished soon after by the Iran-Contra controversy and the White House was preoccupied with damage control. The perception gained ground among Washington insiders that the administration was going to pull back on welfare reform as the One Hundredth Congress got under way in 1987. The president repeated his promise to pursue new welfare legislation in his State of the Union message, but the tone of his message on this subject was muted compared to that of the previous year. His emphasis in 1987, said the president, would be on "a program of welfare reform through state-sponsored, community-based demonstration projects." [26]

Not only did the administration's interest in welfare legislation seem to languish in 1987, Congress was divided on welfare policy. The Senate and the House had different positions. So did interest groups, with most liberal groups taking the position that in the prevailing conservative mood of the country no legislation would be better than any legislation that could get enacted. There seemed to be a log jam. However, a number of factors came together to break this jam.

At the outset of the One Hundredth Congress in 1987, White House aide Charles D. Hobbs, who had led the way in this area, was pushing for legislation to authorize state demonstrations of work-oriented approaches to welfare reform. He drafted legislation calling for the authority to test new approaches involving a wide array of fifty-nine federal government programs to aid the poor that came under the jurisdiction of many different federal agencies and congressional committees. Despite the fact that Hobbs was a participant in crafting what eventually became the Family Support Act of 1988, the act did not highlight such demonstrations. Instead, it consisted of an amalgam of new substantive authorities and funding. A key broker in the Congress in working out the ultimate compromise was Daniel Patrick Moynihan, now chairman of the welfare subcommittee of the Senate Finance Committee.

With the administration still officially supporting welfare reform and Moynihan starting to work on a compromise bill, the spoiler role was initially played by the House. Democratic leaders in the House refused to work with (or even talk to) Republicans. They adopted an ambitious three-year, $7.2 billion bill containing major liberalizations of welfare benefits along with a new program of grants to states for training, education, child care, and other services. The employment and training provisions in this bill were tightly prescribed, engendering opposition by the governors who wanted discretion for the states.

Once the House had acted, Moynihan stepped up his efforts and worked closely with the governors. The Senate enacted a bill that took a middle-ground position between the president and the House. The Senate bill provided flexible grants to the states for welfare employment and training programs, proposed limited benefit liberalizations compared with those proposed by the House, and called for strict requirements for child-support payments by absent parents, mainly of course the fathers of children on welfare.

In the negotiations the bill that emerged closely resembled the Senate bill. Looking across this legislative landscape, one can see that a moderate coalition was formed. A number of factors were critical in 1988, one of them being Moynihan's efforts to forge a coalition. Other important factors were the president's support for welfare changes and the apparent concern of Vice President George Bush (then the Republican presidential candidate) that a veto of a welfare bill would hurt the Republicans in the presidential campaign. Among the governors, Michael N. Castle of Delaware, Bill Clinton of Arkansas, Thomas H. Kean of New Jersey, Michael S. Dukakis of Massachusetts, and Henry Bellmon of Oklahoma played important roles. Three of the five (Castle, Kean, and Bellmon) are moderate Republicans; Clinton and Dukakis are well-known Democrats who were personally and intensely involved in welfare reform efforts at both the state and national levels. The research by the Manpower Demonstration Research Corporation (MDRC) showing that work-welfare programs under the 1981 amendments produced positive results was another factor supporting the consensus on the 1988 act. The MDRC corporation, as will be discussed in the next chapter, tested work-welfare programs in eleven states.

The lead negotiators for the House in fashioning the final bill were Thomas J. Downey of New York for the Democrats, Republican Hank Brown of Colorado, and Dan Rostenkowski, Democratic chair of the

House Ways and Means Committee. Downey chaired and Brown was the ranking minority member of the welfare subcommittee of the House Ways and Means Committee. Senators Lloyd Bentsen, Democratic chair of the Finance Committee, Moynihan, and three Republicans (Minority Leader Bob Dole of Kansas, Bob Packwood of Oregon, and William L. Armstrong of Colorado) played lead roles in the Senate. For the Reagan administration, the chief negotiator was Deputy Budget Director Joseph Wright. Although most liberal groups opposed the legislation, one broke ranks. Work by the Center on Budget and Policy Priorities, ably headed by Robert Greenstein, contributed to the eventual agreement on the key law.[27]

All of the players agreed from the outset on the desirability of one new provision: strengthening systems for collecting child-support payments from absent parents, including wage withholding. Strong backing for these provisions helped build support for a new law. However, this was about the only point on which there was wide agreement from the outset. Many provisions aroused controversy. The major bone of contention in the negotiations was the coverage of two-parent families under AFDC.

Up until 1988, states could at their option include these two-parent families in their AFDC program under what is called AFDC-UP, the letters *UP* standing for the unemployed parents. Moynihan's compromise bill, as did the House bill, would have extended the AFDC-UP program to all states on a mandatory basis. On this issue, however, the administration was adamantly in opposition to Moynihan. Administration officials also showed little interest in Moynihan's grants for state welfare employment programs, JOBS (Job Opportunities and Basic Skills).

Given these and other differences, the table seemed set for confrontation in the closing weeks of the One Hundredth Congress, and many people were surprised when a bill emerged. The key to the agreement was a compromise on the AFDC-UP program. The Democrats in the House and Senate, as I have already said, wanted to make this two-parent program mandatory; the Republicans and the administration did not. The compromise reached was to extend the AFDC-UP program to all states, but with a condition that involved our old friend, CWEP. One parent in all two-parent households was required to work in a community work experience program (CWEP) for at least sixteen hours per week. This provision, which went into effect on a phased basis, was to apply to 75 percent of the AFDC-UP caseload by 1997. This compromise was the handiwork in the Senate of conservative Republican William L. Armstrong.

This CWEP obligation for AFDC-UP family heads was heralded as the reason the administration went along on the final bill. But its impact was likely to be limited; it would affect only a small portion of the total AFDC caseload. It was more of a symbol than an expression of basic agreement between liberals and conservatives. The more important basis for compromise involved the way the concept of "mutual obligation" applied to the AFDC caseload as a whole under Moynihan's JOBS program.

Under JOBS, states are required to achieve a 20 percent level of participation for all eligible AFDC family heads on a phased basis over a period of five years. The JOBS title provides $1 billion in the first four years, fiscal years 1991-1994, for training, education, job search, assessment, and other supportive services and $1.3 billion in the fifth year, fiscal year 1995. The 20 percent participation requirement applies to all welfare family heads who have children three years of age or older. The age stipulation was reached only after considerable debate and compromise.

The 1988 act still contained the authority for CWEP as in the 1981 budget amendments, which means that states can require female welfare family heads to participate in work experience programs.[28] However, unlike the case for two-parent families where federal law mandated up to sixteen hours of participation in a CWEP job for one parent after 1997, the law left the decision as to the nature of the mandate (if any) for CWEP for female welfare family heads up to the states. This means that the participation requirement can be applied to work experience jobs for single-parent welfare family heads but that it is not required. States decide which features of their JOBS program are required. The inclusion of education as an eligible activity under the JOBS program, and the emphasis on going back to school for young welfare mothers, marked an important departure. Another requirement was that states target at least 55 percent of their JOBS expenditures at the "hard-to-serve" part of their caseload, such as unwed teen mothers and longtime welfare recipients.

A close reading of the 1988 Family Support Act suggests that both sides achieved some of their purposes. Liberals won agreement on additional funding for services for AFDC families. They also won on another important point, the extension of child care and Medicaid benefits for one year after a welfare family head enters the labor force and as a result is no longer eligible for cash assistance under AFDC. These are called "transitional benefits." Conservatives also put their fingerprints on the bill where work and mandatory participation are highlighted.

President Reagan signed the Family Support Act with a flourish at a ceremony on October 13, 1988, in the White House Rose Garden, attended by governors and other guests, this author included. The president said the new law would help families achieve "lasting emancipation from welfare dependency." However, before the ink was dry on Reagan's signature, ideological differences emerged over possible effects of the new bill. The law, as I have just indicated, provides one year of "transitional" benefits for Medicaid and child care after an AFDC family head goes to work and earns enough money so that she is no longer eligible for welfare benefits. This provision, which was not a matter for contention in the Congress, quickly emerged as a topic of debate. In an article in the *Wall Street Journal,* which appeared on the very day Reagan signed the bill, conservative welfare expert Charles Murray took aim at this new entitlement, which he claimed would cause more people to enter the welfare system. According to Murray, "Once again, we have adopted a policy on the basis of people who already exhibit the problem we want to solve, while being blind to the effects of the policy on people who do not yet exhibit the problem." [29] His point was that some poor women with children who lose or leave a job, instead of going straight away to a new one, would apply for AFDC, because they would then have one year of Medicaid and child care benefits when they obtained a new job. The architects of the new law were not unmindful of this point; the law directs the secretary of the Department of Health and Human Services to study the effectiveness of the provision for child care transitional benefits and to report back to the Congress.

But Murray was skeptical. He feared we would never roll back these transitional benefits. Rather than studying and eliminating the extended child care entitlement, Murray said it was more likely the transitional benefits would be generalized at some future time to include all families in the affected income categories. Even before this happened, Murray predicted "the number of female-headed families receiving AFDC will increase . . . out of proportion to the general population." Murray's prediction will be hard to assess. If the welfare rolls increase, this does not necessarily tell us that this particular provision of the 1988 law is the reason for it.

The chapters that follow turn our attention to the implementation of the 1981 amendments and the Family Support Act of 1988. Did the troops salute? Did they march?

CHAPTER

4

Studies of the 1981 Changes

At the outset, state governments were slow to pick up on the welfare provisions of the 1981 Budget Act. But despite this hesitant initial reaction, by the middle of Reagan's second term, well before the Family Support Act was passed in 1988, a majority of the states were committed to new workfare employment strategies. As is typical in American federalism, each state put its own spin on its new-style workfare strategy. Almost every state had its own name and acronym for its approach. The Massachusetts flagship program was called ET Choices, ET standing for Employment and Training. The California program was named GAIN, for Greater Avenues to Independence. New Jersey called its program REACH, Realizing Economic Achievement, rhyming with the Georgia program called PEACH, Promoting Economic Achievement. The Michigan program was called MOST, standing for Michigan Opportunity and Skills Training program. The name selected in Arkansas was simply WORK.

There was no broad-gauged implementation study of the 1981 work-welfare amendments. In chapters 5 to 8, I describe the experience of these states, based on interviews I did in five states. But first, this chapter describes studies done on the 1981 work-welfare amendments by the U.S. General Accounting Office, the Congressional Budget Office, and the Manpower Demonstration Research Corporation.

THE GAO STUDIES

The initial studies of the 1981 work-welfare amendments were done by the U.S. General Accounting Office. The GAO is the arm of the Congress responsible for reviewing and auditing federal government expenditures. It has an army of on-site investigators throughout the country. In recent years, the GAO has increasingly used its field staff to conduct evaluations of national programs. At the request of the Congress the GAO initiated a study in 1985 of employment-related programs for applicants and recipients of AFDC benefits. Later it conducted case studies in four selected states.

The 1985 GAO study identified sixty-one work-welfare programs operating under the 1981 Budget Act. This included twenty-five WIN demonstration programs that allowed state welfare agencies to assume sole responsibility for employment programs for welfare recipients. There is disagreement on the significance of this single-state agency authority. Some experts regard it as important; others hold that this shuffling of agency responsibilities does not make much difference, pointing out that most state welfare employment initiatives involved services from a number of agencies. In addition to the twenty-five WIN demonstration programs, the 1985 GAO study identified twenty community work experience (CWEP) programs, six compulsory job search programs, and ten grant diversion (private-sector job) programs. The GAO report on this study focused on welfare employment programs in the thirty-eight states that responded to a survey it conducted. Based on data from these states, it was estimated that 714,000 people (one-fifth of adult recipients of AFDC benefits) were participating in work programs run by state AFDC agencies under the work-welfare provisions of the 1981 Budget Act.[1] Far and away the majority of these people were in so-called WIN-Demo projects.

While the total is impressive, analysts were quick to point out the shortcomings of these data. There were wide variations in how the states defined participation in welfare employment programs. The GAO report stated: "Because participation definitions vary, and some are very liberal, participation estimates are rough and probably higher in

TABLE 4.1
Work-Welfare Program Participation, 1985

Program Type	Number of Participants
WIN Demonstration	681,854
CWEP	19,465
Job Search	36,867
Work supplementation/grant diversion	3,006
TOTAL	714,448

SOURCE: *Work and Welfare: Current AFDC Work Programs and Implications for Federal Policy,* United States General Accounting Office, January 1987, p. 52.

general than the number of people who actually received a service or participated in an activity." [2]

Despite the emphasis in Washington on whether the new programs should be mandatory or voluntary, GAO investigators found this issue was not important at the ground level. The following excerpt from the GAO report is useful to include here in full:

> In the programs we visited, officials tended to view participation requirements as, not a hurdle AFDC applicants and recipients must surmount to receive benefits, but a way to "get people through the door"—people who might not voluntarily participate because of fear, distrust, or lack of self confidence. Once a participant was enrolled, the program often was presented as an opportunity. Program names such as ET Choices, Project Chance, and Options expressed this view. Some programs emphasized marketing to encourage volunteers or convince mandatory registrants that the program had important services to offer. In Massachusetts, for example, outreach literature was mailed and distributed in the community and at job fairs, and the governor held a series of press conferences around the state to honor successful graduates and recruit new participants.[3]

Note the reference to Massachusetts at the end of this passage. Under its ET Choices program this state was aggressive in recruiting participants into its new much-heralded welfare-employment program, despite the fact that its official position stressed the concept of *choices*. AFDC family heads could decide if they wanted to be in the ET program and could choose the track they want to be on—education, training, job search, etc.

Although the mandate issue was front and center in debates about new-style workfare in Washington and in many state capitals, it took on a different cast in practice at the local level. The Massachusetts case is interesting here. In most states, the practice was to talk a good game, but not play one. The work requirement—the stick—was emphasized, but often not brandished, in local welfare offices where services were the main focus.

In the period when Massachusetts began its ET Choices program, resource and administrative limitations effectively meant that the state could restrict its welfare employment services to AFDC recipients who *wanted* to participate. The program was voluntary in a true sense. As a practical matter, the state could only serve the numbers of eligible AFDC recipients who came forward on their own. However, as ET gathered steam and was pushed by Governor Dukakis and other state officials, the supply of motivated AFDC family heads shrank. The state found itself digging deeply into the pool of eligible participants in order to recruit ET participants. State officials often did this aggressively, promoting "hot jobs" and strongly urging AFDC applicants to join ET. As they did this, Massachusetts's official position of "voluntary" participation lost force. This becomes especially clear when one compares Massachusetts with other states that took a strong position in favor of mandatory participation but where the staff of local welfare agencies was unsympathetic to the idea of a mandatory program. Massachusetts's example bears out the key implementation point of my analysis that, despite policy debates about forcing poor people to do things, the reality depends not on words in the law but on the behavior of state and local welfare bureaucracies.

As a follow-up to its first report on the 1981 work-welfare amendments, the GAO undertook a second study analyzing the welfare employment programs of four states. This report, prepared for the U.S. Senate Finance Committee, was issued in January 1988. The four states included two states in which I conducted field interviews. The four were: Massachusetts because of its leadership in the field; Texas and Oregon because they are states represented by the Senate Finance committee chairman, Lloyd Bentsen, and the ranking minority member, Bob Packwood; and Michigan. Michigan was chosen to represent the Midwest and because like Massachusetts it had a prominent welfare employment program in this period.

The Massachusetts ET Choices program was the most expensive of the programs in the GAO four-state sample. The state spent $43 million of its own funds on the program in 1986. Expenditure per placement averaged $3,333.[4] At the other extreme was Texas. That state's welfare employment program provided only job-search assistance. State appropriations to the program were $9 million in 1986; expenditures averaged $457 per placement. The Michigan program was second to Massachusetts in state spending ($33.7 million). Oregon spent $12 million out of its own funds for its program.

The four states in the GAO sample also differed in the amount of federal funds they received for their welfare employment program. Michigan received the most in 1986 ($17 million), followed by Massachusetts ($15 million), Oregon ($8.5 million), and Texas ($6.4 million). Texas is at the bottom of the list, even though it has the largest population and poverty rate among the four sample states. Because Texas has a low welfare benefit (ranking near the bottom in the nation), its AFDC caseload is relatively small, only 2 percent of the state's population as compared to 7 percent in Michigan. If an adult AFDC recipient in Texas finds employment, she is likely to lose all of her welfare benefits. In Michigan (one of the nation's high-benefit states), on the other hand, an AFDC family head who goes to work is more likely to continue to receive benefits and employment-related services.

The Congressional Budget Office (CBO) also issued a report on the 1981 work-welfare amendments. This report drew on the work by GAO and the research of the Manpower Demonstration Research Corporation. The CBO findings are interesting because of the way they picked up on the GAO participation study and the impact research conducted by the Manpower Demonstration Research Corporation. Like GAO, the Congressional Budget Office downplayed the importance of the mandate issue in program operations. The CBO report said that overall states have made considerable use of these new authorities. The report also commented favorably on program effectiveness: "Perhaps the most important finding is that work-related programs, such as job search and training, have repeatedly been shown to be effective in increasing the average earnings of economically disadvantaged female participants, especially those who lack recent work experience."[5] In this latter area, the Congressional Budget Office drew heavily on the studies conducted by the Manpower Demonstration Research Corporation.

STUDIES BY THE MANPOWER DEMONSTRATION
RESEARCH CORPORATION

Established in 1974, the Manpower Demonstration Research Corporation (MDRC), a nonprofit research corporation based in New York
City, has a research staff of approximately one hundred people; its
studies are conducted in cooperation with state and local program
operators. The Corporation initiated demonstration studies in 1983 in
eleven states on the impact of the work-welfare amendments to the 1981
Budget Act. The programs studied included a variety of components—
job search, training, remedial education, testing and assessment, child
care, and in some cases community work experience. The research was
funded with grants from the Ford Foundation, matched with funds
from the participating states or foundations within these states. Altogether, these studies included thirty-five thousand AFDC family heads.

The MDRC studies were focused on individual participants. Their
purpose was to "test what works" for disadvantaged welfare family
heads. The first work-welfare demonstration studied by MDRC was
conducted in San Diego County, California. The results of this study
played a major role in the development of a new policy at the state
level in California in 1985.

The design of the MDRC research is that of a classical experiment.
Corporation officials worked out arrangements with state and local
officials to test specified types of "treatments" under the 1981 Budget
Act. MDRC researchers monitored the treatment. In each site, eligible
welfare family heads were randomly assigned either to a treatment
group of people who participated in the test program or a control
group whose members did not. All the people in the experiment (both
in the treatment and the control group) were informed about the
study; their consent was obtained before they were assigned. If they
were assigned to the control group, they could receive services or
participate in whatever programs were otherwise available to welfare
family heads.

This methodology allowed researchers and the users of the research
to say with confidence whether the work-welfare or other tested programs make a difference in terms of what are known as "dependent
variables." In the case of the work-welfare demonstrations, the dependent variables were the level of employment, wages, and the level of
welfare support. The goals of the treatment were to increase earnings

and hours worked and reduce the level of welfare benefits. Among the main findings from MDRC's studies were:

1. Work-welfare projects had positive impacts, although the size of these impacts was generally modest. The term *impacts* as used here refers to the difference in the amount of time employed, the earnings, and the welfare benefits of the people in the work-welfare demonstration programs compared to persons in the control group.

Using the San Diego study as an illustration, MDRC found that female welfare family heads participating in job search and combined job search and work experience programs had quarterly employment rates between 5 and 10 percentage points above those for the members of the control group, representing a 16 to 40 percent difference. Quarterly earnings gains for persons in the San Diego work-welfare programs averaged between $96 and $213 compared to the control group.[6] Modest welfare savings were also found.

2. Consistent with earlier studies, MDRC found that females who head welfare families made larger employment and earnings gains than male parents in two-parent welfare families.

3. In some of the study states, there was a deterrent effect of work-welfare, that is, welfare rolls declined without a demonstrable associated gain in earnings. This was one of the claimed (actually, hoped for) effects of work-welfare programs on the part of conservatives. The deterrent effect was stronger for males in two-parent AFDC-UP households than for female welfare family heads in single-parent welfare households.

4. Welfare participants with the most serious problems (for example, limited education, limited work experience, early pregnancies, and very low income) tended to register relatively larger earnings and employment gains than those experienced by better-qualified participants. This finding is consistent with what had been learned from earlier studies. The lesson here for employment and training programs is to avoid "creaming." The term refers to selection processes for employment and training programs that favor the most qualified applicants. Many programs that cream have been found to have smaller impacts than those that focus on the most disadvantaged persons. The apparent reason is that the former group (the most qualified people) are likely to get jobs anyway, hence, society is likely to receive greater benefit from programs targeted on the people with the most serious problems.

5. The community work experience (CWEP) jobs provided under welfare employment programs were found to be generally useful. They were not "make-work" jobs, although they were not skilled jobs either.

6. Participants who were surveyed about these work-welfare programs had generally favorable responses and believed the mandatory approach was fair.[7]

One can think of the MDRC studies as taking place in a laboratory where measurements were made of the impact of the treatment being tested. The results of these studies impressed a large number of policymakers and opinion leaders. *New-style workfare works*. It does not achieve large dramatic gains, but it has a consistent, positive impact and its impact is statistically significant. The next question, of course, is: Can new-style workfare be replicated? Can this idea be moved out of the laboratory and be *implemented* on a large scale?

5

Deciding What to Do—the Five State Programs

The implementation process for welfare employment programs in the case-study states in which I conducted interviews is divided into four stages in chapters 5 to 8. The four stages are

- deciding what to do (chapter 5),
- setting up the machinery for doing it (chapter 6),
- program operations (chapter 7),
- evaluating the results, program feedback, and adjustment (chapter 8).

Because the story of welfare employment programs in the 1980s begins with Massachusetts, it is appropriate to start with that state.

MASSACHUSETTS

In 1978, after serving a first term as governor of Massachusetts, Michael S. Dukakis lost his bid for reelection to Edward J. King, a conservative Democrat who became a Reagan favorite among Democratic governors. One of the central issues on which Dukakis and King disagreed was welfare. King favored the narrow "work-for-your-welfare" ideas that liberals disliked in the seventies and can be classified as a hawk on this subject.

In fact the idea that there should be a link between work and welfare began to be put into effect on a pilot basis for male welfare family heads at the end of Dukakis's first term. Charles M. Atkins, who was under secretary in the executive office for human services at the end of Dukakis's first term, developed a statewide plan to reduce welfare spending by placing males on welfare (both in families and on general relief) in public service jobs.[1] In the eighties this was a very popular idea in many states. In the nineties, as welfare policy has become harsher, it has increasingly been favored.

Charles Atkins's 1978 plan did not go into effect because Dukakis lost the gubernatorial election in that year. The first important statement on work-welfare by Governor King after his inauguration in 1979 was the creation of his proposed work and training program, known as WTP. King wanted the state Department of Public Welfare to play an aggressive role in the movement for placing welfare recipients in jobs.[2] His WTP program was launched with fanfare in April 1981. Carried out under the welfare provisions of the new 1981 federal budget act that were the handiwork of the Reagan administration, the program was largely developed and administered by Californians brought in to the state for this purpose. One of King's appointees, Carl B. Williams, had worked on welfare policy under Governor Reagan in California. Williams left Massachusetts at the end of King's stormy term and emerges later on in our story as a principal designer of the GAIN welfare employment program in California developed under Republican Governor George Deukmejian.

Governor King's WTP program quickly became controversial because of the vigorous way sanctions were applied to welfare family heads who failed to adhere to its requirements to seek, accept, and maintain employment as a condition of their eligibility for public assistance.[3] (The program stipulated that eligible welfare family heads who did not fulfill the requirement to participate in WTP would lose the portion of their AFDC benefits representing the share of the grant intended to meet the needs of the family head.) Welfare advocates in Massachusetts concentrated their attack on the procedures that required welfare recipients to go to welfare offices to be processed for job referrals. They contended that these referrals were often to employment offices a long distance from the residence of the welfare families. If the head of a welfare family failed to respond, the sanctions process was initiated immediately. Over 5,000 persons were referred for sanctioning under WTP in 1983, and 1,636 of those referred were sanctioned.[4]

The WTP program was constantly under fire. Opponents of its sanctioning process challenged and eventually derailed the program in court. This issue, in fact, played a major role in King's failure to win reelection in 1982 when Michael Dukakis won the Democratic gubernatorial primary and was elected to his second term as governor. Shortly after the new Dukakis term began in 1983, the courts administered the coup de grace to WTP. In *Rheault v. Spirito* (Spirito was King's welfare commissioner), the court ruled against the King program, forcing the state retroactively to restore benefits denied under the WTP sanctioning provision.[5]

The *Rheault v. Spirito* decision, however, did not cause the second Dukakis administration to turn its back on the idea of linking work and welfare. In April 1983, at the outset of Dukakis's second term as governor, his new secretary of human services, Manuel Carballo, met with leaders of public and nonprofit human services organizations to discuss welfare job programs. After the meeting, Carballo appointed a task force, not to abolish WTP but to restructure it.[6] The task force recommended a substitute program, one that also emphasized work as an alternative to welfare. The new design involved a series of sequential training and educational steps in the form of options for program participants "designed to support and motivate, rather than sanction and punish." [7]

At about the time that the Carballo task force submitted its report, Charles Atkins, who had served in the governor's office in the first Dukakis administration, returned to state government as the commissioner of public welfare. He accepted this position with the understanding that employment and training reforms would be his top priority assignment.[8] Atkins's philosophy was to sell rather than sanction. He viewed the welfare agency as staffed by "bank clerks." Atkins sought to change both the image and operations of the agency.[9]

Atkins, who is a principal figure in the implementation story in chapters 5 to 8, had a special interest in management. He placed emphasis on the theories put forth by Thomas J. Peters and Robert W. Waterman, Jr., in their book about good managers in the corporate sector, *In Search of Excellence*. Peters and Waterman advocate, among other ideas, "MBWA," which stands for Management By Walking Around. In an interview in 1988, Atkins said his impression from his first visit to the welfare office in Roxbury (the most distressed area in the city of Boston) was that it was like a war zone. He said he needed an escort of armed guards. "The clients were ready to burn the place down." [10]

Atkins and his associates developed the state's new welfare employment program with the central theme of "Choices." The new program was put in place through administrative action rather than legislation. Under the ET (Employment and Training) Choices program, the state offered an array of services to AFDC family heads. Representatives of the providers of the services, to the extent possible, were to be located in the offices of the Department of Public Welfare, and the offices were to be refurbished. Atkins recruited a new central staff. His slogan was, "Send the Californians back to California." The ET program set specific performance goals and set up new systems for marketing to promote jobs and services and to monitor for results.

> The new Employment and Training (ET) Program is a comprehensive employment program for AFDC recipients which is committed to providing them with the opportunities and motivation for economic self-sufficiency and long-term employment. The Program is based on positive incentives, and it offers a wide variety of program components and support services suited to an individual's needs. Other features which are designed to make ET successful are the emphasis on coordination with other state agencies, single state agency management, and positive marketing techniques. [11]

The goal of the ET program was to place people in jobs that would "get them out of poverty." The regulations required that clients could not be referred to jobs paying less than five dollars per hour. (This hourly rate was raised to six dollars in 1988.) Participants could receive free or subsidized day care for their children for one year after taking a job that ended their welfare eligibility. ET participants were also eligible for extended health care coverage for two years under the state Medicaid program, Commonhealth.

Most services provided to welfare recipients under the Massachusetts ET program (training, education, testing and assessment, child care, remedial education) are not directly administered by the Department of Public Welfare. They are contracted out to other public agencies, nonprofit groups, and private organizations. The main interagency relationship under ET was with the state's employment and training agency, assigned the tasks of providing job placement and most training services. At the outset of ET, Massachusetts had a special advantage in cementing this interagency relationship. Atkins's wife, Kristen Demong, headed the employment and training agency for the first four years under the ET program. The expectation, not an unreasonable one, was that the two departments would work well together, which they did. This solved a problem that in many states had been a long-standing barrier to the implementation of welfare employment goals.

To pull together the Massachusetts story, the liberal political values on social issues that we associate with Massachusetts, and the way Governor King's WTP program bumped up against these values, were underlying factors in the decision to highlight voluntarism under Dukakis's successor program. The controversies that confronted Governor King, Carl Williams, and the other Californians recruited by King to help him launch the WTP program set the stage for Michael Dukakis and his team—Manuel Carballo, Charles Atkins, Kristen Demong, and others—to chart a new course. Atkins came to his post with a strong interest in management and stayed with the ET Choices program for six years. Economic conditions contributed positively to the quick start-up of ET; the state's economy was strong when the ET program went into effect; and it was easier to obtain the needed resources and to place clients in jobs in a tight labor market. Structural factors were also important. The state controls and manages welfare programs in Massachusetts, in contrast to two of the other states I studied—California and New Jersey—which have state-supervised, county-administered systems. In both of these states, tensions resulting from this shared responsibility between levels of government (state and county) were a major barrier to the implementation of new-style workfare.

CALIFORNIA

The link between welfare and work has had an important history in California state politics. Ronald Reagan in the seventies, like Michael Dukakis in the eighties, rose to national attention in large part because of his welfare policies. This issue continued to be highly salient in California and, in fact, is still a hot potato of California politics.

A decade after Reagan's welfare reforms were adopted in 1971, another conservative governor, George Deukmejian, made welfare reform a high priority. Deukmejian proposed a State Training and Employment Program for Unemployed Parents (STEP-UP) in 1983, aimed at providing job search and work experience for welfare recipients on a mandatory basis statewide. His proposal was similar in tone and substance to King's WTP program in Massachusetts. Initially it was rejected by the legislature, but it touched off a policy debate that eventually resulted in legislation creating the GAIN (Greater Avenues to Independence) program enacted in 1985.

The debate about STEP-UP and, later, GAIN centered on differences between the governor and the legislature. Deukmejian took a conservative position highlighting the work requirement and mandatory community work experience (CWEP) for persons who could not be placed in regular jobs. On the other side, key participants in this debate were Arthur Agnos, a Democratic assemblyman who was elected mayor of San Francisco in December 1987, senators Diane Watson and William Green, and other liberal members of the legislative and social action groups. On the conservative side, key players in addition to the governor were David B. Swoap (secretary of California's health and welfare agency), Charles Hobbs (who later worked in the Reagan White House), and Carl B. Williams (just returned from his Massachusetts service under Governor Ed King). Swoap, the leader of this group, had been the director of welfare when Reagan was governor of California; he had also served in the interim as deputy secretary of the U.S. Department of Health and Human Services in Washington during the Reagan administration.

The relatively equal strength of the opposing forces resulted in a two-year stalemate. At one point in the running debate in the legislature, it was decided that the two groups (the Agnos group and the Swoap group) should together visit other states to learn about welfare employment programs. Two states with polar positions on the mandate issue were selected for field visits: Massachusetts and West Virginia. West Virginia took a strong prowork position stressing community work experience. The delegation also visited Pennsylvania, which had recently adopted a mandatory work experience program for two-parent welfare families and people receiving state general assistance payments.[12]

Agnos, Swoap, and associates made their field visits in 1984. Their main reactions, not surprisingly, divided along ideological lines: the Agnos group favored the Massachusetts approach, at least on paper, and the Swoap group favored the officially more obligatory approach of West Virginia.

An incident that occurred on this trip became a symbol of the conceptual differences between the two groups. When the Californians were visiting West Virginia, they toured a water treatment plant and met a woman named Velda Jenkins. In her mid-thirties with three children, Velda Jenkins was on AFDC because her husband was in prison. She was assigned to a work-experience job in a water treatment facility. The managers of the West Virginia work-welfare program boasted that she was being trained as a water quality tester. But there was a hitch. During the two years she had been assigned to the water treatment plant, there had been a budget squeeze and Jenkins had spent her time not as a water tester but mopping floors. She had complained about this assignment, but nothing had been done to change it.[13] Based on this incident, the phrase "Velda factor" became a shorthand descriptor often used in California welfare debates to describe the work-relief issue: Should a welfare family head be required to accept any job, even a dead-end, low-wage position? Although the two sides differed on this issue, there was common ground.

Swoap came away from these field visits with a positive view of community work experience as an important step in the work-welfare process. "We got a consistent sense from recipients in these jobs, even in jobs that at first glance were not very interesting, that they were glad to be out doing something."[14] Despite the fact he was concerned about the Velda factor, Agnos softened his view on this issue. He said: "We saw it repeatedly through West Virginia, people doing things they didn't necessarily like, saying 'if they hadn't made me do it I wouldn't have done it, but it's better than doing nothing at home.' That was when my feelings of opposition to the mandatory feature started to change."[15]

The difference in attitude between the Swoap and Agnos forces on community work experience produced a Solomon-like compromise that resulted in elements of both viewpoints being embodied in the Greater Avenues to Independence (GAIN) program in 1985. For liberals, there were requirements for a series of often-expensive services (testing, assessment, education, training, etc.) modeled on the Massachusetts program. For conservatives, there was the requirement that eligible AFDC family heads participate in GAIN, including community work experience for family heads who did obtain a regular job through the earlier steps in the GAIN process.

The GAIN law spelled out this political compromise in enormous and tedious detail, including both an elaborate sequence of services and an equally elaborate sanctioning process. The law required that counties follow the exact sequence of services in the law in administering the new program. As it turned out, this elaborate political bargain became a major hurdle in the implementation of the GAIN program. According to Health and Welfare Secretary David Swoap, the GAIN program "incorporates a unique blend of what traditionally have been considered 'liberal' and 'conservative' attitudes toward caring for the poor." [16] The essence of this California treaty of work-welfare is the "mutual obligation" concept mentioned earlier, whereby the state is obligated to provide services and the welfare recipient is obligated to participate in these services. The form this policy bargain took under the GAIN program is spelled out in a formal "social contract" (available both in English and Spanish) signed by both the case manager and the recipient.

Structure matters. The elaborate sequence of steps written into the California law, and the fact that in California county governments administer welfare payments and services, produced an implementation challenge of near epic proportions.

In sum, a comparison of the main features of the California decision process shows that the history of welfare policy in California, like Massachusetts, involved a tug-of-war between liberals and conservatives, with the conservatives having more clout in California than in Massachusetts. On the conservative side, Ronald Reagan was the first leader of the band in California; he was followed by George Deukmejian, David Swoap, Robert Carleson, Charles Hobbs, and Carl Williams. On the liberal side, Arthur Agnos was the strongest leader. When he was elected mayor of San Francisco, a number of his colleagues in the legislature (especially Senators Diane Watson and William Green) picked up the cudgels for liberals. Economic conditions played basically the same role in California that they did in Massachusetts. In 1985, when the GAIN law was passed, the California economy was in relatively good shape. The labor market was tightening and the state government considered itself in a position to support new initiatives. Substantial state funds (in this case nearly $500 million per year) were provided for GAIN.

NEW JERSEY

New Jersey's welfare employment program, enacted in 1987, was named REACH (Realizing Economic Achievement). Chronologically it followed California; substantively it was closer to Massachusetts. Under ET in Massachusetts, clients are only obligated to register. (Actually, this is a federal government requirement.) The decision of what services they will participate in, if any, is up to them. New Jersey's program, in contrast to Massachusetts, requires participation in a service component of REACH. But the formal difference between California and New Jersey, which moves New Jersey back toward Massachusetts on the new-style workfare employment continuum, involves one particular service, community work experience (CWEP). In California, participation in the sequence of services spelled out in the law includes community work experience for persons who cannot be placed in regular employment. The New Jersey program, however, does not require the counties to include a community work experience component, although counties can do so at their option.

Adding the New Jersey version of new-style workfare to this examination helps us bring out two additional points. One involves the way the policy was adopted. In California and New Jersey, laws were enacted chartering the state's new-style workfare program, whereas in Massachusetts the program was established administratively under existing law. A second important point of comparison involves the role of the governor. Like Governor Dukakis in Massachusetts, Governor Thomas H. Kean in New Jersey took a much stronger out-front position in this area than Governor George Deukmejian in California. Kean, a more liberal Republican than Deukmejian, strongly backed legislation to charter New Jersey's welfare employment strategy. By contrast, Deukmejian, who tended to draw back from GAIN, often seemed unsure about his state's program because of the costs involved.

Governor Kean served in this period as chairman of the committee on human resources of the National Governors' Association and had first hand knowledge of the Massachusetts and California programs, having visited both states. In the spring of 1986, he launched the planning process for welfare reform and recruited Drew Altman as the new commissioner for the state's Department of Human Services. Altman had formerly been a foundation official and a federal official in the health field. Kean instructed Altman to give welfare reform top priority. The REACH plan, presented in Kean's 1987 State of the State address, was described as "the nation's first welfare reform to touch every welfare recipient in a major state." The reference here is to the fact that the New Jersey program required participation in REACH for all eligible welfare family heads whose youngest child was two years old or above. (The cut-off was six years of age in Massachusetts and California, in this respect following the current national law, which was changed to three years in the Family Support Act of 1988.) In his 1987 State of the State message, Kean stressed the mutual-obligation theme of REACH, asserting that welfare recipients have a "moral responsibility" to work, but that the state must "remove the barriers that prevent welfare recipients from becoming independent." [17]

Kean's plan, which many of the state's newspapers described as "workfare," was greeted favorably at the outset. Editorials hailed it as a way to end welfare, saying it was overdue no matter what the cost. A statewide poll showed 70 percent in favor of a work requirement for welfare family heads with children two years or older if the state provided child care.[18] As the season wore on, however, liberal groups increasingly attacked the REACH plan, and the legislature began to put up roadblocks. The research office of the legislature issued a report described in the press as "ripping" Kean's plan, asserting that it "is riddled with overstated savings and understated costs." [19] Some Democratic legislators called for a test program limited to a few counties. Despite this opposition, the governor prevailed. Legislation authorizing a statewide REACH program was enacted in September 1987.

Although on paper Massachusetts, California, and New Jersey can be arrayed on a continuum in terms of the degree of obligation imposed (Massachusetts at one end and California on the other), legal requirements, as we have seen, take on a different character in the implementation process. Under the Massachusetts program, the signal that "work is good for you" was transmitted with gusto in the implementation of ET. This was especially the case after the ET program had been in effect awhile and the pool of people to be dealt with came to include harder cases in terms of the employability of clients. At first it was easy to find volunteers. However, as the pool of volunteers was used up, ET Choices under Dukakis increasingly involved strong pressure on welfare family heads to "choose" ET. Workers avidly promoted jobs and their associated services, notably child care and health care. On the other hand, in California and New Jersey the obligation to participate in new-style workfare was presented by officials in many counties in a way that can be described as lukewarm, even hostile.

There were a number of reasons for this coolness toward the REACH participation requirement in New Jersey, among them resistance on the part of the welfare bureaucracy, the state-county structure for welfare, which limited the state's leverage to influence the welfare bureaucracy, and the lack of resources to assist all of the people who came within the net of the REACH program. The essential point, once again, is that the policy-making process operated at a level of abstraction that made the mandate issue appear to be more important than it actually was in implementation.

In sum, a number of positive factors worked in favor of the REACH program. The history of welfare policy in New Jersey was not as controversial as in Massachusetts and California; fiscal conditions in the eighties were favorable for the adoption of work-welfare and other new social policies in New Jersey; the governor, Altman, and others cared about this new approach; and labor market conditions were conducive to the new policy. On the other side, the structural factor stands out as the big negative. New Jersey's tradition of local home rule had a strong effect on the effort to implement the REACH brand of new-style workfare.

MICHIGAN

In Michigan the adoption of a new welfare employment program in the eighties was less of an event and more evolutionary and low key than in the states described so far. The state's own history of welfare employment programs begins by noting that the U.S. Congress had pushed in this direction since the 1960s. It then describes a series of state programs established to comply with different national laws, beginning with the 1962 Community Work and Training Program under Kennedy.[20] After Community Work and Training came the Title V work experience program under the Economic Opportunity Act of 1964, part of Lyndon Johnson's War on Poverty. Title V was sponsored in the Congress by Representative Carl Perkins, then chairman of the House Education and Labor Committee. It was known as the "Happy Pappy program" because of its emphasis on work experience for men in rural areas, such as Perkins's Kentucky congressional district. Michigan picked up on each of these laws in turn.

In 1967 Michigan adopted a Work Incentive program (WIN) under the law enacted that year, which two decades later was superseded by the JOBS title of the Family Support Act. State officials in Michigan attributed the "low level of performance" under WIN to the program's emphasis on training as opposed to job placement and also to the recession of 1967. In 1972 the WIN program was amended by Congress. The work requirement was strengthened in connection with the debate over Nixon's Family Assistance Plan. Michigan again responded, calling its new program WIN II. Later in 1975, the two federal agencies responsible for WIN (the departments of Labor and Health, Education, and Welfare) issued new regulations for WIN, and Michigan officials once again redesigned their WIN program.

Under the Reagan administration, Michigan continued to follow the federal lead. It was one of the first states to respond to the work-welfare provisions of the 1981 Budget Act. The state established an Employment and Training Program (ETP) in 1982, which assigned exclusive responsibility for work-welfare to the welfare agency as a "WIN-demo" project.[21] In 1984, the state remodeled and renamed this program, setting up a single employment program for all employable Department of Social Services clients.[22] This program merged the employment programs for AFDC and general relief recipients. The new program was named the Michigan Opportunity and Skills Training Program (MOST). At the time it was adopted and put into effect, MOST was frequently mentioned in the national press as one of the country's notable initiatives under the 1981 Budget Act to advance new-style workfare. Later, its reputation tended to fade as other states gave more public prominence to their versions of the new-style workfare ideas of the eighties.

The story line in Michigan is that MOST was not so much a new program as old wine in a new bottle. Its distinguishing characteristic, compared to its preceding ETP program, was that MOST also covered the general assistance caseload. (Michigan is one of a handful of states that in 1984 had a state-administered general assistance program for people not covered under the AFDC program.) There was little hoopla in Michigan in 1984, no new legislation for new-style workfare and no prominent administrative rearrangement when the MOST program succeeded ETP. There appear to be a number of reasons for the low-keyed approach in Michigan. One is that Michigan's history of high unemployment reduced people's expectations about what could be accomplished under a program to get people off of the welfare rolls. In fact, during the 1980s much of the attention of welfare planners in Michigan was on issues other than employment preparation and job placement as was the case in Massachusetts, California, and New Jersey. A 1988 report to the governor from a blue ribbon commission on welfare addressed jobs and job preparation but said the funding for these programs was limited. The report was not upbeat about prospects for these programs:

Michigan simply does not have enough state and federal money to provide employment, training, and transition support services to all welfare clients who need them. Today, for example, while all Michigan welfare recipients are required to register for the MOST program, the state can afford to have only a third of these registrants participate. Even if the federal government goes ahead with one of the "reform" proposals currently being considered by the Congress, it is unlikely that dramatic increases in funding will follow.[23]

Although unlike Massachusetts, California, and New Jersey it was business as usual in Michigan, on a closer look business as usual in Michigan is impressive. The reference just quoted to "only a third" of the registrants being able to participate compares favorably with the numbers in other case-study states. In 1986 Michigan spent almost as much as Massachusetts on welfare employment yet had more participants and a higher monthly participation rate. The state devoted $12.4 million to MOST as compared with $20.3 million in state funds allocated for ET in Massachusetts. (Massachusetts, according to the GAO, spent more per participant than Michigan—$1,257 versus $410.)

Program data for MOST from the period of my field research reinforce this point about the relatively high activity level of MOST. For the nine months of October 1987 through June 1988, 30.7 percent of the registrants were active in MOST—90,826 participants. A wide range of services was provided. There were over 17,000 people in education and vocational training, 1,000 in on-the-job training, 15,000 in high school, 2,000 in remedial education, and 9,000 in community work experience.[24] Looked at in these terms, the Michigan record is nothing to sneeze at.

Moreover, Michigan, unlike New Jersey and California, does not face the same hurdle of having to operate welfare job and training programs through county governments jealous of their prerogatives. As in Massachusetts, welfare programs in Michigan are the responsibility of the state government. Each county (eighty-three in all) has a social services board with two members appointed by the county government and one by the governor. The county welfare director (not a member of the social services board) is appointed by the state director of social services. In the larger counties, such as Wayne County (which includes Detroit), there are several local offices; in others only one. Altogether the state has 115 welfare office directors, who report to 6 zone managers who are state employees.

Summing up for Michigan, the mood of MOST in Michigan was

more subdued than in the other case-study states; MOST was seen as another step in a succession of welfare employment programs. Likewise the values underlying MOST were less controversial at the state level than in the other states studied. The work requirement and the idea of community work experience were not hot issues in Lansing (the state capital), although this is not the same as saying everyone in the system was on board. The people and organizations who administered MOST were not, at least as far as I could tell, that different from the people who had had these kinds of responsibilities at the state, county, and local levels beforehand. Economic conditions in the late 1980s were better than in the early 1980s; thus there was a heightened level of expectation for MOST. The social policy setting in Michigan involves a decided difference between Detroit, the local site I visited, and Flint and the rest of the state, because of their serious urban problems.

My field visit to Detroit brings out an important point: even in states where the state government is in charge of welfare there is great variation in what happens in local offices. I visited three high-concentration welfare offices in Detroit in March 1989. In the first office, the idea of a work requirement and the assignment of people to community work experience were seen as "last resorts" for problem cases. This reflects the official theory of the MOST program that CWEP should be used only in those cases where persons have limited work experience and skills and would benefit from experience in the labor force that will help them become accustomed to dealing with the requirements of regular jobs.

Very different positions were taken by workers in the other two welfare offices I visited. In one office, sanctions and CWEP taken together were viewed favorably—actually with enthusiasm—by welfare workers as the best approach for welfare because workers there said they believed that recipients as a group need to be pushed. ("They need to be taught responsibility.")

All the way over at the other end of the spectrum, the MOST workers in the third Detroit local office regarded sanctions and CWEP highly unfavorably. They saw them as "punitive and unfair." They said they did everything they could to avoid having responsibility for administering these features of the MOST program. They said that in their view unless and until work-welfare programs and services are truly effective and universal, it is unfair to single out some recipients for sanctions and CWEP. The evidence suggests that this third position is widely shared by local welfare agency personnel. The delicate policy balance of MOST, GAIN, or REACH may sound fine in the governor's office, but it comes up against hard sledding at ground level. This was true both of state-administered and state-supervised systems in the states I visited that had the most extensive new-style workfare programs under the 1981 budget amendments.

ARKANSAS

Among the case-study states Arkansas had a more limited, but very cost-effective, new-style workfare program in the eighties despite the fact that the state was one of the first states in its region to introduce changes to carry out the purposes of the work-welfare amendments to the 1981 Budget Act. Throughout this period, Arkansas Governor Bill Clinton was a highly involved and visible leader, nationally pressing for reforms to expand welfare employment programs.

Arkansas inaugurated its work-welfare program under the 1981 Budget Act as a WIN-Demo project in October 1982 and shortly afterward joined as one of the eleven states in the demonstration study of state work-welfare programs conducted by the Manpower Demonstration Research Corporation. (California, among the other case-study states, also participated in the MDRC research.) Later in July 1987 Arkansas launched its statewide program, WORK. On paper the WORK program resembled the California and Michigan programs. Participation was mandatory. The plan called for a community work experience (CWEP) component. The idea of the program was to make connections among services—education, training, child care, transportation—to enable AFDC single-parent family heads (the state did not have an AFDC-UP program prior to 1989) to go to work and exit from welfare. Like New Jersey, Arkansas received a waiver to enable its WORK program to focus on young welfare family heads, those with children three years of age or over. This was done on the theory that these younger families are less "settled in" on welfare than other families.[25]

The big difference in Arkansas compared to the other four states examined is the actual operation of the WORK program. Spending for this purpose was limited. In an environment in which money for other social programs was also scarce, the Arkansas WORK program involved mainly job search and referral to other programs. Moreover, the record for making linkages with other programs, particularly training programs, was checkered.

Eligible recipients under the Arkansas WORK program were supposed to be called in for assessment, and if they were found eligible, referred to a "job club" (group job search) followed by a period of individual job search. In its evaluation MDRC said: "Well-run group job search sessions or job clubs, aided by a central manual—but less clearly defined individual search components—characterized the WORK program." [26] The MDRC study, based on two counties (Pulaski and Jefferson), found that enrollees "were rarely assigned to work experience." [27] These findings square with those from my field visits to the state, where the dominant theme of interviews with state officials and local welfare workers was limitations of resources.

At ground level, the personnel for the WORK program expressed few doubts about the mandatory character of the WORK program or the idea of having a work experience component. In fact, I was surprised by a common theme in these interviews—the need for a stronger sanctioning process. Workers complained that the drawn-out sanctioning process, involving multiple notices and long waiting times, made it very difficult for them to give substance to the work focus of the new program.

To sum up, welfare personnel in Arkansas appeared to have a strong commitment to new-style workfare. The organizational structure where the state controls the administration of the welfare system is an asset, although relations with service-providing agencies were said to be a problem, especially in the case of job training and child care services. In addition to coordination problems, and actually towering over them, the factors that stand out as barriers to the execution of new-style workfare in Arkansas were the availability of resources and economic conditions.

6

Program Start-Up

On the basis of a close look at two of the sample states, Massachusetts and New Jersey, the experience of program start-up for new-style workfare programs described in this chapter reveals a lot about the barriers leaders face in attempting to achieve enduring changes in the behavior of public bureaucracies.

Governor Dukakis and his appointees had more success in general in pushing the ET idea into the system than did Governor Kean and company in New Jersey. A major reason for this is that the entire welfare system was under state control in Massachusetts. In New Jersey, on the other hand, despite the fact that the governor and his top officials were strongly committed to REACH, the structure of state-local relations made it difficult to manipulate and change the welfare system from the top down. In fact, the problems involved in setting up the machinery to implement new local programs caused Governor Kean to propose to the legislature in February 1989 that the state take over the welfare system in order, among other reasons, to be able to implement policy changes like REACH more easily.

Over the long haul the trend in the United States has been to adopt more centralized state welfare systems as in Massachusetts. Many states have now taken over full responsibility for the AFDC program, whereas under state "supervised" welfare systems, the state sets policy and pays part of the cost of welfare benefits and services but the main responsibility is in the hands of the counties and sometimes towns. Where this system remains, counties have wide policy and administrative latitude and tend to have a strong parochial feeling about "their" programs. In 1989, the ratio of state-administered to state-supervised welfare systems was two to one for the nation. Thirty-five states administered the AFDC program directly. Eligibility workers and social workers in these states are state employees. Fifteen states had state-supervised systems. The employees of welfare agencies, including those working on welfare employment programs, work for county government.

MASSACHUSETTS

Since Massachusetts was the first state to march down the welfare employment road in the 1980s and the governor and other state officials aggressively promoted the program, ET Choices attracted widespread national attention. Because of this, the Ford Foundation asked Robert D. Behn, a professor of political science at Duke University, to conduct a management study of the start-up of the ET program in Massachusetts. This section draws heavily on Behn's work, along with my own interviews.

A major theme Behn emphasizes is *flexibility*. Like Massachusetts welfare commissioner Charles M. Atkins, Behn draws on the management strategy of Thomas J. Peters and Robert H. Waterman, Jr. In their book, *In Search of Excellence,* Peters and Waterman use the military metaphor "ready, aim, fire." Their purpose is not to advocate such steplike action but rather to say that excellent companies rarely have the opportunity to proceed in such a logical fashion. They experiment; they are flexible. The more appropriate metaphor, according to Peters and Waterman, is "aim, ready, fire."

Paraphrasing Peters and Waterman, and arguing that there is an even more fast-changing environment in government, Behn says the management style of the Massachusetts welfare department was "aim, fire, ready." His reason for shifting the metaphor one more notch is to convey the need to adjust as one goes along in public policy implementation. Commissioner Atkins and other top executives of the Massachusetts Department of Public Welfare knew what they were aiming at—getting welfare recipients off of the rolls and into jobs. But when they started ET they were not ready. They fired anyway. Then they got ready. In the first year, says Behn, ET was "an extremely primitive program." He adds, "ET was designed to operate statewide from day one. It was not a pilot project to be tested in a few, select offices. Thus the question was not *whether* the program would work. The question was *how* to make it work. Atkins's managerial philosophy was clear: 'Get it up and running, and then fix it.' " [1]

This point about flexibility in the implementation process parallels the widespread theory of public policy formulation, which holds that policy-making is *incremental*. According to Aaron Wildavsky and Angela Browne, "implementation is *exploration*. Any political body that argues otherwise mistakenly regards itself as omniscient and omnipotent." [2] Using the Wildavsky-Browne metaphor to focus on implementation, top agency managers who serve at the pleasure of the person who appointed them are explorers. They cannot be sure exactly where they are going, much less how to get there. The good ones are alert to the need to change the course along the way. Even when they are quite sure where they are headed, they have to be prepared for surprises that may require changing the trip plan.

Referring to the way the ET program was put into place, Behn said it was "experimental." The top officials learned from experience. "Atkins knew where he wanted to go but not how to get there. So Atkins started groping along." [3] "Groping" is Behn's favorite metaphor: "Despite years of experience and study, even the best manager must grope along. He tests different ideas and gauges their results. Then he tries different combinations and permutations of the more productive ideas. Rather than develop a detailed strategy to be followed unswervingly, a good manager establishes a specific direction and then gropes his way towards it." [4]

The management team that set up the ET program in Massachusetts was composed of Atkins's people. They were appointed by him, came into the state government in many cases because of the ET program, and understood, admired, and shared Atkins's management philosophy. Atkins, a graduate of Dartmouth College, received a masters degree in physics from Yale and did postgraduate work in political science and economics at the Massachusetts Institute of Technology. He had previously served as a management consultant for the Arthur D. Little Company and had had tours of duty in Washington and the New York City government before coming to Massachusetts. Atkins and the other key agency officials who set up the ET program had something else in common that is rare in government—relative longevity in office. This core management group for ET stayed together for a considerable amount of time. Atkins left the commissionership in February 1989, six years after launching ET. Two of his principal associates for ET left a short time before that; the last one (deputy commissioner Jolie Bain-Pillsbury) left shortly after Atkins.

Prior to coming to Massachusetts, Atkins had been deputy to New York City Health Services administrator Gordon Chase. Chase, who taught public management at Harvard and Brandeis universities, was the managerial guru of the men and women who ran the ET program. When Chase died in an automobile accident, both Governor Dukakis and Atkins spoke at his memorial service. Atkins recited Chase's ten management principles, which so dominated Atkins's own management philosophy. As commissioner of the Department of Public Welfare, Atkins was always ready to hand out the list of Chase's ten principles.

1. Chose carefully what is doable, decide whether you can accomplish something substantial, and then set your goals.
2. If you are unable to meet your goals, change them.
3. Recruit a first-class staff and derive first-class benefits.
4. Understand that it is output that counts.
5. Be able to quantify results. If you can't find a way, you haven't tried hard enough.
6. Report on your progress to your superiors.
7. Keep yourself well informed on important projects.
8. Schedule periodic meetings with program managers to get results firsthand.
9. Praise your staff.
10. Remember that government has the will and capacity to deliver services efficiently to people in need.[5]

The first two points in the Chase coda about setting goals and revising them when needed fit Behn's description, already cited, of the start-up of ET. Reflecting Chase's third principle, Atkins placed emphasis on recruiting a "first-class staff." He also stressed measurable goals (principle numbers 4 and 5). Another key to Atkins's management style (number 9 on Chase's list) is "praise your staff." This is a principle that Atkins carried to its highest power. As the ET program was put in place, he constantly gave out award certificates and frequently arranged for Governor Dukakis to do so as well. Behn's book tells this part of the story.

> During the first five years of ET, the Massachusetts Department of Public Welfare was full of hoopla. Atkins, Glynn, Pillsbury, and Burke-Tatum actively pursued endless excuses to give out rewards. For example, on August 28, 1986, the department held a ceremony at the State House to "Celebrate the Success of ET CHOICES." Fiscal year 1986 was the first year in which all of the local offices achieved their ET totals, and Governor Dukakis was on hand to present the director of each local office with its ET award—which is displayed in the lobby of the office, just as similar awards are displayed inside any McDonald's. All the "winners" had their picture taken in front of a big banner saying "Thank You for a Job Well Done" while holding their awards and flanked by Atkins and Dukakis. These pictures make it not only into a frame on the office wall but also, with a little help from Lee Chelminiak, the department's director of communications, into the local newspaper.[6]

In the spirit of this passage, the Massachusetts Department of Public Welfare under Atkins was a pioneer in bringing public relations skills to the fore in social policy, an area in which this is rarely done and even more rarely done well. Howard Waddell, a former social worker who turned out to be a skilled public relations expert, was discovered by Atkins early in the ET start-up period. He was put in charge of what became an in-house advertising agency to change the image of welfare. Waddell viewed his work as being like selling life insurance; he stressed success stories presented at a level accessible to a wide audience in order, he said, to give ET "a personality."[7]

As Dukakis's second term began and ET was made a top priority, Atkins set about recruiting a staff to implement the new program. Virtually all of the top staff came from outside the department. His deputy, Thomas Glynn, was the principal management strategist for ET. Glynn had been a community organizer and a staff assistant to Massachusetts Governor Francis W. Sargent and Congressman Michael Harrington. Previously, he had served in executive positions in Washington and had received the Ph.D. degree from the Heller School of Social Welfare at Brandeis. It was Glynn who took the lead in shifting and reformulating ET goals at the beginning of each annual policy cycle. ET, said Glynn, "was a different program every year; it sustained itself by changing."[8] In an interview, Glynn cited approvingly the metaphor used in Behn's report—"aim, fire, ready"—and added that "change gets people to think about what they are doing."[9] Glynn stressed two other management strategies: (1) the use of an organizational chart as a way to let people know who's in charge and what was happening to top staff and (2) the importance of setting and monitoring numerical goals for the placement of ET participants in jobs. Goals were posted everywhere and trumpeted when they were achieved. They were tied to important aspects of the experiences of ET participants, especially wage rates and job retention. Atkins and Glynn first set goals they thought could be achieved (everyone likes success) and then ratcheted them up as the management capacity of the ET program increased.

Another top member of the ET team was social work professional Barbara Bourke-Tatum, whose area of expertise was employment and training. She had a strong hand in both the design and start-up of the ET program and also in figuring out how to get the message across to participants that the goals and rules of welfare had changed. Bourke-Tatum emphasized the need to influence the mind-set of agency employees. In our interview, she talked about "changing the hearts and minds of the workers on ET in the department's fifty-six local offices." [10]

Atkins, Glynn, Bourke-Tatum, and Jolie Bain-Pillsbury constituted the core management team for ET. Bain-Pillsbury was in charge of local office operations. She organized the offices into clusters, each of which reported to a program manager. Her strategy was to divide up the Boston offices and assign them to clusters that included suburban areas and small towns. Her reason for this was to motivate the urban offices to achieve standards of performance met by offices all across the state. Fortuitously for ET, Atkins and Bain-Pillsbury were able to increase the salaries of the local office managers at the outset of the program under a state law that allowed this to be done by administrative action in the first year of Dukakis's reentry term.

Behn uses another idea from Peters and Waterman in assessing the start-up for ET, namely that good corporate management systems have "simultaneous loose-tight properties." The phrase refers to the system's looseness in the sense that its managers are entrepreneurial in terms of the way they do their job, and to its concurrent tightness in the sense that "corporate leaders insist on a few key values that define the firm's mission." Good managers, according to Peters and Waterman, "develop an organizational culture that supports and reinforces those values." [11] Behn sees the opposite practice as usual in the public sector.

Unfortunately, management as practiced in government often takes the inverse approach. All too frequently, public management is characterized by *tight-loose* properties. Government is tight about implementation, but loose about its mission. In part, this may be inherent to government, reflecting several important differences between government and business organizations. But it also reflects some specific attitudes towards government that have developed in the American culture.[12]

To sum up, the management system for ET when I visited in 1988 and 1989 reflected a philosophy that stressed flexibility, placed trust in carefully selected key staff, emphasized the fulfillment of measurable performance goals, and hammered away at good public relations. Massachusetts stands out in these terms among my case-study states for the cohesiveness of the central staff and the strength of Atkins's top-down management style. The core group for managing ET stayed together for five years and was strongly backed by Governor Dukakis who regarded this program as one of his top priorities. When Atkins left in March 1989 after six years in the commissionership, only one of the top agency officials for ET, Jolie Bain-Pillsbury, was still at the department. Reinterviewed in March 1989, Bain-Pillsbury used the metaphor of "turning an ocean liner" to express her hopes about sustaining the changes made under ET. Because it takes a long time to turn a large ship when it is taking a new course, said Bain-Pillsbury, it is likely to stay on the new course; implementation is incremental and reversing a step-by-step management-development process cannot be done abruptly or suddenly. New ideas, once they penetrate a public bureaucracy, continue to influence its operations, or at least this is what Bain-Pillsbury hoped. She believed that the selection and deployment of local office managers committed to the new direction for the agency was the key to the longevity she hoped for the ET idea.[13]

NEW JERSEY

Although some observers refer to New Jersey as the nation's "most urban" state, in reality it is *sub*urban. The state has 567 cities and towns. Most are relatively small; many are bedroom communities for the two large cities that abut the state, New York and Philadelphia. The political system and culture of New Jersey place a premium on "home rule" for local governments. The state also has a number of distressed cities that stand out for the gravity of the urban problems they face, although their share of the state's total population is small, less than 15 percent and declining. Relations between these troubled cities (Newark, the largest city in the state; Camden, the most distressed city; and Trenton, Jersey City, New Brunswick, Paterson, and East Orange) and the better-off suburban communities produce the most sensitive and confrontational issue of state policy in New Jersey. This issue between the "haves" and "have-nots" infuses the state's politics; the state's welfare program is often the symbol of this issue. In December 1987, New Jersey had 120,000 AFDC families consisting of 365,000 individuals and 96 percent of its welfare families were headed by women. The caseload is concentrated in the state's distressed cities.

Among the new-style workfare programs in my case-study states, the one I know best is New Jersey's REACH (Realizing Economic Achievement) program. I was living in New Jersey at the time, teaching at Princeton University, and I was involved as an adviser in the planning for REACH. The Manpower Demonstration Research Corporation (MDRC) also had a hand in the REACH start-up. During this period, and continuing while I was writing this book, I chaired the board and was active in the work of MDRC. MDRC was also involved in studying the California GAIN program.

The most interesting lessons of the start-up of new-style workfare in New Jersey involve the federalism dimension of government in the United States. The task of setting up the machinery for New Jersey's REACH law was assigned to the state's Department of Human Services headed by Commissioner Drew Altman. The law called for the rapid start-up of the new program, with the goal that it should be "fully operational" in all twenty-one of the state's counties within three years. This decision on the target date for REACH implementation reflects the political calendar. Governor Thomas H. Kean was in his second term in 1987 when the REACH law was enacted; the next gubernatorial election was to be held in 1989; and the next governor would take office in January 1990. Governors in New Jersey are limited to two consecutive terms. This meant that if the Kean administration wanted to make its mark with REACH, the program would have to be pretty well entrenched by the time the new administration came on the scene. In its planning for REACH, the state contracted with MDRC to provide technical assistance. Based on the corporation's experience in other states, particularly California, MDRC experts cautioned state officials about the time-consuming nature of setting up a new welfare employment system and warned that the initial phase-in schedule was overly optimistic.

The state phased in a county's REACH program, first by approving its plan, which often involved intensive state-county negotiations. State officials began with three counties—Bergen, Middlesex, and Union. These counties were slated for state approval and program start-up in October 1987, one month after the new law was enacted. Two counties—Mercer and Passaic—followed four months later. Five more were to start up four months after that, and plans were for them to be followed by five counties in May 1988, three more early in 1989, and then the eight remaining counties. The three counties accounting for the largest caseloads and representing the toughest implementation problems—Essex (which contains the city of Newark), Camden (which contains the city of Camden), and Hudson (which contains Jersey City)—were initially assigned to the January 1989 group. All of these plans had to be modified, the longest delay being due to problems in Essex County.

Within each county, the plan was to sign up welfare applicants first, followed by the current welfare recipients. The state developed guidelines but told the counties its intention was to be flexible. Very much in line with the theme of this book, the hardest part of the management challenge posed by the REACH program was to get county welfare departments to behave in new ways. There were many delays and problems, both in approving county plans and in working with the counties after their plan was approved. Although some county governments were sympathetic to REACH, the politics of the state-county relationship in New Jersey are confrontational, almost no matter what the issue is. This deep-rooted adversarial presumption permeates the state-county relationship, working against policy changes, even when state and county officials share the same goals.

Three things—money, policy discretion, and publicity—make up the intergovernmental currency in New Jersey. County officials have learned from long experience that if they dig in their heels, no matter what the issue, they are likely to be given greater freedom to act and more money to do so. Each county was a new challenge; each issue a new issue. Planners who think that a template for new policy can be used interchangeably, as in this case from county to county, are bound to be frustrated. There is no "cookie-cutter" way to implement new state policies in New Jersey or, for that matter, in many other situations involving federal-state and state-local relationships. Even when deals were struck and plans agreed to, the REACH implementation process moved slowly and often in unexpected ways. At the end of the first full year of REACH (July 1, 1988, to June 30, 1989), it was estimated that REACH spending would be $13 million (40 percent) less than originally projected. Among the reasons given for this shortfall were the later than anticipated and more difficult and deliberate phase-in of the three largest urban counties; the heavier than estimated reliance on in-home day care, which costs less than center care; and the lower than anticipated spending for training-related expenses, particularly transportation.[14] Changes were made in the state guidelines in this period to deal with emerging issues and assuage county concerns, including procedures for case managers to expand outreach for center day care, provide transportation for orientation and assessment periods, and revise the start-up plans and goals for urban counties.

Although the state-county relationship dominated the start-up within New Jersey, the bargaining that took place at the outset of the new program also involved hard bargaining sessions in Washington over the waivers of federal law needed for the REACH program. Waivers were needed to establish a lower age-limit for children (families with children two years of age or older) and to adopt a formula for federal-state cost sharing for the new services. This latter issue of cost sharing required Governor Kean to use his clout in Washington in often tense negotiations. Federal officials took the position that the REACH plan had to be cost-neutral vis-à-vis earlier programs; questions about what this really meant were not easily resolved. Human Services Commissioner Drew Altman, who had worked on previous waiver issues as a federal official, said, "this was the most difficult thing I have ever been involved in." [15] Governor Kean met twice with President Reagan, who assured him that the necessary waivers would be granted. Nonetheless, foot dragging by the U.S. Office of Management and Budget continued until the green light was given just hours after the law establishing the REACH program went into effect.

Once the waivers were in place, the state of New Jersey (the supplicant in this Washington-Trenton federalism relationship) turned around and became the grantor of benefits to counties. And, as noted, the counties in their time-honored way tried to use the full measure of their leverage to get the most out of this bargain.[16] It was not just the state and counties that were players in this game. County welfare agencies had to make deals with public and nonprofit social service agencies from whom they needed to obtain components of REACH—education, training, child care, testing, assessment, job counseling, placement, transportation, health, etc.

Several people played key roles in setting up the machinery for REACH in New Jersey. Governor Kean made the program a top priority of his second term, placing the full weight of his office behind the enactment and implementation of REACH. As commissioner of human services, Drew Altman brought a strong policy-oriented management style to bear and emphasized REACH as one of five gubernatorial policy initiatives for his department.[17] As his principal associate for implementing REACH, Altman recruited Dennis Beatrice, who had formerly served as the administrator of the Massachusetts Medicaid program and taught courses in social policy at the Heller School of Social Welfare at Brandeis. In turn, Beatrice drew on the efforts of people who had been in the agency prior to the arrival of Altman and Beatrice, Michael Laracy and Eileen McGinnis.

Altman and Beatrice viewed the challenge of implementing REACH as a constant process of "reinventing REACH to fit its complex environment."[18] They described stages in setting up the new program. The first involved getting agreement on a formula for the program that would win over enough of the critical actors to get it through the legislature. This, they found, required "overbuilding" the program, making it so elaborate that in retrospect the program that was legislated was "not a program that could be implemented." The governor and Altman found that they had to incorporate the diverse ideas of major players, especially members of the legislature and interest groups, to put together a coalition for their plan. Later, they paid a price for some of the bargains they struck and had to backtrack to undo them.[19]

According to Altman and Beatrice, the initial start-up for REACH was based on the legislative design, yet as they proceeded, the program had to be changed. This required what they called a second "fix-it" phase in which the program was redefined in negotiations with county governments and provider groups. In the spring of 1988, the department issued a policy memorandum that modified REACH by simplifying the sanctioning procedures, raising the amount of voucher payments for child care, permitting a slower phase-in of the current AFDC case-load, providing funds to the counties for their data systems, and appointing a special committee to reduce paperwork and streamline the intake procedures.

Within the New Jersey Department of Human Services, the responsibility for the REACH program was assigned to an ad hoc coordinating group. Dennis Beatrice, working with Michael Laracy and Eileen McGinnis, drew on work of thirteen subgroups composed of agency personnel from the major parts of the department. This coordination system differs from the Massachusetts approach in which the top management structure of the welfare agency was reorganized and new people were appointed to implement ET. In New Jersey, time constraints and political barriers were seen as requiring the coordination approach. The tradeoff here involved speed of getting going versus depth of managerial penetration. Beatrice's core group for REACH could get into gear more quickly than would have been the case if new line managers had been appointed. But this meant that the people working on the implementation of REACH did so on a temporary basis, and in some cases their commitment to the new program and their job status was tenuous.

Two main problems stood out in the start-up period for REACH—assuring client flow and job placement. The design for REACH envisioned the continuous movement of participants through the system, but as Dennis Beatrice observed in the fall of 1988 (one year into the program) "people kept getting stuck all over the place." [20] Remedies had to be devised to overcome obstacles that caused delays. Even more important, the top agency officials found that although local agencies and officials were receptive to providing services they balked at job placement. They preferred to view REACH as a service program for people *in the system* rather than as a way to get people *out* of the system. It is at points like these that the leadership factor makes the biggest difference; what is involved, as I stressed in the case of Massachusetts, is changing the mind-set and behavior of the bureaucracy.

The staff for REACH at the state level had bargaining leverage with the counties in the form of money for staff, facilities and equipment, child care, training, education, and other services. Moreover, state officials were not without allies. They found, for example, that at the end of the pipeline, when it came to the critical role played by case managers in knitting together services, there was a lot of support for the new program in many counties.

Far and away outdistancing issues related to the goals and structure of the REACH program, the issue that dominates the New Jersey REACH start-up story is the state-county relationship. Governor Kean could have taken another route to overhaul welfare in New Jersey from the outset. He could have used the institution of REACH as a reason for taking over welfare altogether, which many county officials (particularly county executives, legislators, and budget and general administrative officials) would have liked, because their county government would no longer have had to pay the cost sharing for welfare allocated to the counties. (Counties pay one-quarter of the state share of AFDC and half of the state's administrative costs.) Such a state takeover was not proposed in 1987 because state officials felt it would take too much time and be too disruptive. The governor and his key appointees believed they would not be able to put the REACH program into effect if they had to use the time and political muscle necessary to win enactment of a state takeover. Sixteen months later, however, they had a change of mind.

In his 1989 budget message, Governor Kean told the legislature that he favored a state takeover of welfare as part of a plan to reduce the reliance of local governments on property taxation. The state's experience of implementing the REACH program was one of the factors in this decision. Within county governments, welfare agency heads and the heads of related social agencies were not sure how to react to this proposal. County and labor union officials who opposed a state takeover faced a dilemma. If they took a foot-dragging stance on REACH, they ran the risk of playing into the governor's hands, in effect, strengthening the argument for a state takeover. If instead they pushed harder to implement REACH and build up the prestige of the program, they risked losing their usual leverage with the state on budget, personnel, and management issues. Surely, this federalism two-step of no and then yes to state takeover was unplanned. However, it may have been the wisest course. First get the game started. Then use the threat of a state takeover to stimulate the players to greater effort at halftime.

Four years after I started my fieldwork on new-style workfare in mid-1988, the policy terrain of welfare in New Jersey was more turbulent than when I began. Earlier, I described a 1992 Senate hearing chaired by Daniel Patrick Moynihan on a controversial new law that replaced REACH with a program that is in many respects similar to it but nonetheless sought to signal a break with the past. The new law requires new county policies and federal waivers, thus once again churning up federalism issues at both the federal-state and state-local levels. Such policy shifts are not unusual in emotionally tense and unsettled areas of social policy such as welfare; they underline the theme of this book, which is how hard it is to carry out social policy. They make the tough jobs of implementation even tougher.

7

Program Operations

Policy debates are full of arguments about the types of new programs that should be adopted and how they should operate. But there is a dearth of good information on how they *actually do* operate. Undertaking this book, I was concerned that I would not have enough of a knowledge base from which to dig into the dense underbrush of program operations in order to draw conclusions about how a given new state work-welfare policy affects the welfare bureaucracy and other public agencies in their day-to-day operations. Fortunately, a rich in-depth study of the implementation of the welfare-employment program in California was conducted by the Manpower Demonstration Research Corporation. This study of California's Greater Avenues to Independence program (GAIN) provides a large body of information for a huge state. The state has one-sixth of the nation's AFDC caseload, and the GAIN program, which is comprehensive and ambitious, had a budget that exceeded the amount spent by any other state on a new-style workfare initiative in the mid-eighties.

THE MDRC CALIFORNIA EVALUATION

Beginning in March 1986, shortly after the GAIN law was passed, the state government of California entered into a contract with the MDRC to do a three-part evaluation of the new program. The evaluation included, as a first step, an implementation study of the GAIN program as it was being put into effect. The implementation study was based on three main sources of data: (1) field research on the implementation process; (2) the results of a survey of GAIN personnel in selected counties; and (3) an examination of case files for a participant-flow analysis.

The other two parts of the MDRC evaluation, both of which are considered in the next chapter, are: (1) a study of the impact of the GAIN program on individual participants; and (2) a cost-benefit study. The individual-impact analysis was conducted in six counties, which randomly assigned some persons to GAIN and others to a control group. The justification for the decision to use this experimental design for an impact evaluation of a new program was that it would not be possible, even if a county wanted to do so, to serve all eligible GAIN participants at the outset of the program.

The first report on the MDRC-GAIN implementation study was issued in March 1987. It described the planning process at the state level and in counties with the earliest state-approved GAIN plans. The second implementation report, issued two years later in April 1989, took the story further; it presented detailed information about the start-up and operation of the GAIN program in eight of the first ten counties to implement the new program. The eight counties represent a cross section of California counties. As shown in table 7.1, two have small AFDC populations and are agricultural counties; four are middle-sized (2,000 or more GAIN registrants); and two are larger, more urban counties with over 10,000 GAIN registrants. Altogether, the eight counties accounted for 14 percent of the state's AFDC caseload.

As it turned out, the difference in size among the counties was found to be an important indicator of differences in the way the GAIN program was implemented. Small counties made the most progress in carrying out the GAIN program. Unfortunately for purposes of implementing new-style workfare, not all counties are small. Among California's 58 counties, one county stands out in the scale of the challenge represented by the GAIN program and, in fact, towers over the others.

TABLE 7.1
Total Number Gain Registrants by County in the Second GAIN Implementation Report by MDRC

County	Total Registrants
	December 1987
Napa	419
San Mateo	890
Butte	2,285
Ventura	2,293
Kern	2,597
Stanislaus	2,620
Santa Clara	12,736
Fresno	14,786
TOTAL	38,626

SOURCE: James Riccio, Barbara Goldman, Gayle Hamilton, Karin Martinson, and Alan Orenstein, *GAIN: Early Implementation Experiences and Lessons,* and Manpower Demonstration Research Corporation, April 1989, p. 25.

Los Angeles County has seven times as large an AFDC caseload (200,000) as Fresno, the county in the sample for the MDRC-GAIN implementation study with the largest AFDC caseload. Los Angeles County accounts for one-third of the total state AFDC caseload. Compared to the other case-study states considered in this book, Los Angeles County's AFDC caseload is roughly equal to that of the state of Michigan; it is more than twice as large as that of Massachusetts and nearly twice as large as that of New Jersey.

FINDINGS FROM THE MDRC-GAIN IMPLEMENTATION STUDY

When the research for the second MDRC implementation report was completed, the GAIN program had been in effect for almost three years. The second report covers sixteen to twenty-four months of program operations. At a minimum it includes an examination of six months of client-flow data for a sample of individual registrants who enrolled in GAIN in late 1986 and the early part of 1987. The sample includes both single-parent and two-parent welfare families, called AFDC-U in California, with the *U* standing for the unemployed status of the parents. As shown in table 7.2, the total sample for the participant-flow part of the MDRC evaluation was 2,098 persons (sample sizes columns added together) who were required to participate in GAIN and 429 persons who volunteered for the program.

In addition to the participant-flow study based on the analysis of case files, MDRC conducted a survey of the attitudes and activities of welfare department personnel one year after program start-up. Five hundred and fifteen workers were interviewed, with a 95 percent or better response rate in all but one of the eight counties. These data were supplemented by two to three weeks of on-site field research in each of the sample counties. For the field research, both formal and informal interviews were conducted with welfare agency staff and staff members of the providers of GAIN services, such as community colleges, the employment service, job training programs, child care agencies, and adult schools.

The GAIN program departs from past experience in California in two ways. The law requires continuous participation of all eligible participants. Second, it is highly specific about the sequence of the services to be provided and the stepwise series of sanctions in cases of nonparticipation.

THE PARTICIPATION FLOW

At the outset of GAIN, California officials and MDRC directed their attention to the ambitious participation objective of the GAIN program. The law envisions that all eligible AFDC family heads (those who are able-bodied and have children six years of age or over and where child care is available) would move continuously without any downtime from one GAIN component to the next until they were regularly employed and ultimately would leave the welfare rolls. There is widespread public support for reducing the welfare rolls this way. The state backed this vision up with large appropriations of its own funds. Its intent was to break with the past under the WIN program, where large numbers of people were not served but were instead assigned to a "holding pool" that stagnated.

What happens when politicians decide to make changes such as these? Clearly this continuous-participation goal would be difficult to achieve. The participant-flow data for the second report on the MDRC implementation study of the California GAIN program was for a period of at least six months; in four of the sample counties, the report contained up to or more than twelve months of follow-up data.

TABLE 7.2

Participant Flow Follow-Up Periods and Sample Sizes

| County | Last Date of Data Collection | Range of Months in Follow-Up Period[a] | Total Number of Registrants During Sample Enrollment Period | | | Percent of Registrants Sampled | | | Sample Sizes | | |
| | | | Mandatory | | Voluntary[b] | Mandatory | | Voluntary[b] | Mandatory | | Voluntary[b] |
			AFDC-FG	AFDC-U	AFDC-FG	AFDC-FG	AFDC-U	AFDC-FG	AFDC-FG	AFDC-U	AFDC-FG
Butte	12/31/87	7–10	531	307	N/A	26.9	50.2	N/A	143	154	N/A
Fresno	9/30/87	6–9	1423	1112	N/A	10.1	13.5	N/A	144	150	N/A
Kern	10/31/87	7–11	859	765	N/A	17.2	19.5	N/A	148	149	N/A
Napa	1/31/88	7–13	86	50	141	100.0	100.0	100.0	86	50	141
San Mateo	2/29/88	8–12	319	84	108	49.2	90.5	100.0	157	76	108
Santa Clara	11/30/87	6–9	1754	1088	624	8.0	12.0	14.6	141	131	91
Stanislaus	2/29/88	8–12	611	602	N/A	23.4	25.1	N/A	143	151	N/A
Ventura	11/30/87	7–12	986	475	142	15.0	26.7	62.7	148	127	89
All counties			6569	4483	1015	16.9	22.0	42.2	1110	988	429

NOTES:

[a]The first month of the follow-up period does not include the month in which an individual initially registered.

[b]Only volunteers in Napa, San Mateo, Santa Clara, and Ventura were used in the research.

In summary, the results of the participant-flow analysis reveal three roughly equal groups. One group required to register for GAIN did not participate. Although referred to the program, the people in this group did not show up for the orientation meeting, which is the first step in the GAIN process. Half of the people in this group were later deferred or deregistered. The second group did attend orientation but did not participate in any GAIN service (job search, education, training, etc.). Most of these people were deferred from GAIN because they were working, they were ill, or they had a "severe family crisis." The third group participated in orientation and also participated in a GAIN component. Of this group, 11 percent participated on what was defined by MDRC as "a continuous basis," that is, they were active in a GAIN component for at least 70 percent of the days in which they were registered for the program. The MDRC report contains an excellent summary diagram (figure 7.1) that shows these three outcomes for one hundred typical AFDC single-parent family heads eligible for the program. The heavily outlined boxes in the diagram represent the three major groups just described.

How should these results be viewed? Are they good or bad? Both positions can be taken. The second MDRC-GAIN report summarized the results as follows:

> The eight study counties were generally successful in developing the network of education and training services called for by the GAIN legislation. It is more difficult to assess the counties' achievement in implementing the program's mandate that certain welfare recipients participate in GAIN services. For example, during the six-month follow-up period, 78 percent of GAIN registrants were, for at least part of this time, in statuses consistent with GAIN's provisions: they had either participated in an activity or, by the end of this period, were not required to do so because of employment or other reasons. But the other 22 percent of registrants were not covered by one of these statuses during that period, although staff had initiated GAIN's enforcement procedures with a portion of them . . . While over three-quarters of the registrants had reached an authorized program status during this period, about one-third of all registrants (34 percent) attended a GAIN activity. Substantially fewer participated on a continuous basis during the time they were registered for the program. Almost all of those who did participate engaged in basic education or job search, or continued in approved education or training activities begun on their own before entering GAIN.[1]

FIGURE 7.1

Participation Patterns for One Hundred Typical AFDC-FG Mandatory Registrants Within Six Months of Registration

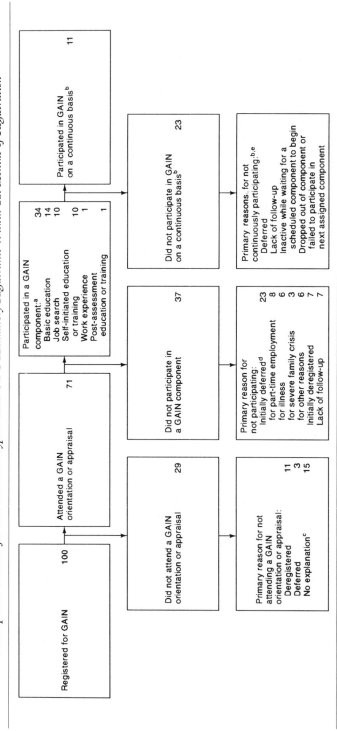

SOURCE: One hundred typical members of MDRC's participant flow sample.

NOTES: Fresno is not included because of unavailable data.

[a]Registrants can participate in more than one component.

[b]Registrants were considered to have participated on a continuous basis if they were active for at least 70 percent of the days during the period they were registered for the program. "Other reasons" included no information explaining why these registrants did not attend a GAIN orientation or appraisal.

[c]GAIN case files included no information explaining why these registrants did not attend a GAIN orientation or appraisal.

[d]Registrants can defer more than once for different reasons; only the reason for the first deferral is shown. "Other reasons" include lack of transportation or child care; emotional, mental, or legal problems; temporary job layoff; "soft" mandatory status (registrant was attending school and had a child under six); alcoholism or drug addiction; and illegal alien status.

[e]Information on why a registrant did not continuously participate was not collected for this study; thus no breakdown of the number of registrants by specific reason is given.

One idea that can be derived from this summary analysis is that the bottle is three-quarters full, as stated in this quotation from the MDRC implementation study. MDRC evaluators found that 78 percent of the people who were required to participate in GAIN either did so or were deferred or deregistered. Readers of this book who have a healthy respect for the institutional and intergovernmental barriers to program change in this field, as I do, are likely to be impressed with this finding. On the other hand, critics could point out—and did—that of the people originally assigned to GAIN, two-thirds either did not participate or attended an orientation session and then did not do anything after that. Conservative critics have also pointed out that in this MDRC study, participation in the GAIN program is defined as being active for one day in a GAIN component. As noted, a relatively very small percentage (11 percent) of the people in the sample participated in GAIN for 70 percent of the days they were registered in the program.

COUNTY POLICY DECISIONS

As in New Jersey, the federalism dimension of implementation of new-style workfare in California posed major challenges because of the divided responsibility between the state and the counties. Welfare is state supervised and county administered in California. The first step for GAIN was the development of a county plan, which had to be submitted and approved by the state Department of Social Services. As it turned out, state approval presented a substantial obstacle. The process was slow and cumbersome. Plans languished in Sacramento. County officials complained about this bottleneck and what they saw as the state's unwillingness to assign a sufficiently flexible role to the counties in getting the GAIN program under way.

The development of a service network is the heart of the county plan. The eight counties in the sample for the MDRC implementation study assigned different roles to different agencies and types of workers. MDRC's description of the range of program styles and approaches provides a good picture of what took place. The assignment of service responsibilities is the key variable at the local level. Many different patterns are possible involving the role of the welfare department, community colleges and adult schools, the employment service (called the Employment Development Department in California), and the agencies responsible for administering the Job Training Partnership Act (JTPA). The Job Training Partnership Act is a federal law that provides funds to the states with requirements about the kinds of training that can be provided and also the types of people who can participate. Around the country there is great variation in the organization of JTPA services and their relationship to other public agencies and programs. Since JTPA services are required to be targeted on the disadvantaged, there is a logic to close linkages (even joint operating arrangements) with the welfare system. However, there are also features of the federal law that pull the other way. The JTPA law calls for a reporting system that can be used to assess programs and allocate funds on the basis of performance. Performance is primarily defined in terms of getting people into jobs. In many states, the employment service, which is also federally aided, competes with welfare agencies, viewing welfare recipients as hard-to-employ and hence likely to make it more difficult for JTPA agencies to achieve high performance.

There is wide variation in JTPA-welfare relationships. In Napa County in California and also in some counties I visited in Michigan, the two programs operate on a completely integrated and combined basis. In Napa County most GAIN activities, including day-to-day case management for the movement of people through the sequence of services, was subcontracted to the JTPA agency.[2] This consolidated GAIN-JTPA model has the virtue of merging the streams of people receiving publicly subsidized employment and training services. An added advantage of this approach is that it removes the stigma of welfare. Potential employers do not know whether a person who is trained or referred is a welfare client or not. But the bureaucratic barriers to such mergers, as I have noted, are formidable. The JTPA and welfare systems operate under different laws and are overseen from Washington and the state capital by different agencies with different aims and constituencies. On paper the idea of such a merger has strong appeal. In operation it is very hard to do. It is probably significant in this connection that Napa is the smallest county in the California GAIN sample, both in population and in caseload size (population 106,000; caseload for GAIN, 419).

Under GAIN the county welfare agency is the agency that in most cases organizes and operates a network of providers for a range of different types of services. The alphabet-soup picture of how this works is shown in table 7.3. The table shows the major service components of GAIN for each of the counties studied and the agency assigned to provide the service. The large role assigned to JTPA in Napa County is shown in the first column. The role of the county welfare department (CWD) predominates in most of the other counties.

As for particular services, job search was fairly evenly split between the welfare agencies doing it with their own staff and subcontracting it out to the employment service. Basic education in California was mostly provided by adult schools. Assessment of job readiness and training needs was mostly performed by the JTPA agency, as was the provision of vocational and training services. Community colleges in California also had a major role in vocational education and training. For community work experience (called PREP in California), the predominant assignment was to the welfare agency. Child care referral agencies, either separately or along with the welfare agency, were responsible for locating child care and placement.

In addition to its distinctive organizational structure, Napa stands out among the sample counties for the upbeat tone of its GAIN program. Orientation sessions were positive and individualized, stressing "barrier bashing." Early on in the establishment of the GAIN program in Napa, special efforts were made to teach the county's eligibility workers, who perform the intake and clerical services for the welfare system, about the aims and services of GAIN. They were invited to breakfast meetings where they were briefed on the new program. Caseloads per worker were found by MDRC researchers to be relatively low, seventy-one cases per worker in Napa.[3] The county, in addition, has a relatively simple service network—one adult high school and one community college.

When GAIN staff were asked about their relationship with clients, 92 percent in Napa said they were "excellent."[4] This is the highest rating among the sample counties. (Note that this finding represents a response by twelve out of thirteen respondents who rated their relationship with clients as "excellent.") At the other end of the spectrum, Kern County had the lowest satisfaction ratings for client-staff relationships and in many respects is the mirror image of Napa in the style and tone of its GAIN program. One of the survey questions asked in this part of the study was whether the agency sets a "tough tone" with clients. In these terms, Napa and Kern were polar opposites. None of the workers in Napa said this was what the agency sought to do. Nearly half of the respondents (seven out of fifteen) said this was the aim in Kern County. The second lowest rating on this "tough tone" question was for Santa Clara County, the most urban county in the

TABLE 7.3

Distribution of Responsibility for Selected GAIN Services Between County Welfare Department and Other Agencies, by County

GAIN Service	Napa	San Mateo	Butte	Ventura	Stanislaus	Kern	Santa Clara	Fresno
GAIN registration	CWD	CWD	CWD	CWD	CWD	CWD	CWD	CWD
Orientation and appraisal	JTPA	CWD	CWD	CWD	CWD	CWD	CWD	CWD
Selecting service providers for registrants	JTPA	CWD	CWD	CWD	CWD Other	CWD	CWD	CWD JTPA
Monitoring and enforcement	JTPA	CWD	CWD	CWD	CWD Other	CWD	CWD	CWD JTPA Other
Providing job search services	JTPA	EDD	CWD*	CWD	CWD	EDD	EDD	CWD
Providing basic education services	AS**	AS CC Other	AS CC	AS**	AS CC Other	AS	AS Other	AS Other
Providing assessment services	JTPA	JTPA Other	JTPA CC ROC/P	CC	Other	CC	JTPA**+	JTPA CC ROC/P

Providing vocational education/training services	JTPA CC ROC/P Other	JTPA CC Other	JTPA CC ROC/P	JTPA CC ROC/P	JTPA CC ROC/P Other	CC JTPA Other	JTPA CC Other	JTPA CC ROC/P
Developing PREP positions	JTPA	CWD	JTPA	CWD	Other	CWD	CWD	CWD
Assistance in locating child care	R&R	CWD R&R	CWD R&R	R&R	CWD R&R	CWD R&R	CWD R&R**	CWD R&R

SOURCE: Field interviews.
NOTES: CWD = county welfare department
AS = adult school
CC = community college
R&R = child care resource and referral
ROC/P = Regional Occupational Center/Program
JTPA = Job Training Partnership Act agency
EDD = Employment Development Department
Other = Other agencies

*EDD staff assist welfare department staff during the first week of job club.
**Staff from the outside agency performing this function are *colocated* with the GAIN program.
+Two different JTPA agencies provided this service.

sample, where seven of the forty GAIN staff members surveyed (18 percent) said the agency wants to set a "tough tone" with clients.

This point about the tone of the program is important, though hard to measure, and the sample sizes here are small. Overall, however, the combination of the participant-flow, observational, and attitudinal data in the MDRC-GAIN report gives us a picture of what is involved in changing the signals and services of welfare bureaucracies. Do people get served? Do they stay in the program? Do GAIN workers stress jobs and getting people off of welfare? Do they believe the purpose of the agency has changed? Tables 7.4 and 7.5 from the MDRC second GAIN implementation report show the attitudes of GAIN workers in the counties studied. In particular, table 7.5 on staff perceptions of the goals of the GAIN program shows considerable county variations in underlying philosophy and attitudes, although on the whole it indicates a substantial internalization of the goals of the GAIN program. There were some important differences. Note the variation in staff perceptions of the goal of reducing the stigma of welfare (item 4). This goal as well as the goal of improving staff-client relations (item 6) were generally supported by the staff, but there are appreciable differences in their opinions as to the relative emphasis given to these goals in the different counties.

THE ROLES OF LOCAL PERSONNEL

The two main groups of agency personnel for GAIN are eligibility workers and case managers. The former have predominantly clerical and data-handling roles related to determining and administering welfare payments. In all but two counties (Fresno and Napa), eligibility workers had a limited role in GAIN. In Napa County, as mentioned earlier, a special effort was made to bring eligibility workers on board as part of the GAIN system. The second MDRC-GAIN implementation report includes a table of answers by eligibility workers to four questions about their attitude toward GAIN. Except on one question, eligibility workers in Napa County rank highest in ways that demonstrate support for the goals of the GAIN program (see table 7.6). Only in Napa did eligibility workers indicate a substantial increase in their job satisfaction due to the GAIN program.

The fact that in most counties MDRC researchers found that eligibility workers did not have a high level of knowledge of the GAIN program presents a problem. If eligibility workers, as welfare gatekeepers, have relatively little sense of ownership of the GAIN program, they are not likely to do a good job at intake in explaining the dual themes of the new system of mutual obligation: requirements and opportunities. Eligibility workers are also important to the ongoing monitoring of GAIN participants. It is their job to report on the activities and changes in status of the people required to participate. Such reports of status information are critical to the operation of GAIN, both for service participation and for the sanctioning process when a person registered for GAIN does not participate. If eligibility workers see GAIN as just more paperwork (see table 7.6, next to last line), and as a result treat it as just another hoop recipients have to jump through, it is hard to make credible the idea that GAIN is special. On the whole, MDRC found that "eligibility workers in most counties were not well informed about GAIN and tended not to promote the program to registrants." [5]

An exception to this generalization was Fresno County in the initial period of the GAIN program. In Fresno County (population 606,000), eligibility workers were assigned primary responsibility for the new program at the outset of GAIN.[6] This was based on the "program planners' belief that GAIN services would be effectively institutional-ized if they were directly linked with the primary activity of the agency." [7] However, with caseloads for eligibility workers of 150 registrants per worker, this experiment proved to be short-lived; increasingly, GAIN functions were turned over to case managers in Fresno as in the other counties studied by MDRC.

Throughout the country one of the most important aims of new-style workfare, both under the 1981 Budget Act and under the Family Support Act of 1988, has involved new responsibilities for case man-agers. A lot of ink has been used to say what case management is supposed to mean in this context. The "case management model" is essentially one in which a service expert has a counseling, scorekeeper, gatekeeper, and tracking role to assist employable welfare family heads and their families. Ideally, this involves more than assessment and referral; it includes advice on appropriate and accessible services for the family heads and their children on a basis that is workable in terms of scheduling and transportation and also takes cognizance of other family needs—for example, health, family planning, and housing.

It is ironic that in the sixties this model was the predominant organizational approach, although not so employment-focused. Each welfare family head in the sixties was assigned to a social worker whose

TABLE 7.4

GAIN Staff Perceptions of Welfare Recipients, Staff Morale, and Relationships with Registrants, by County

Survey Item	Napa	San Mateo	Butte	Ventura	Kern	Stanislaus	Santa Clara	Fresno GAIN	Fresno EW[a]	Total
Percentage high on perception of welfare recipients scale[b]	85%	84%	88%	54%	40%	56%	63%	50%	32%	63%[c]
Percentage high on staff morale scale[b]	77	84	83	50	27	92	65	80	30	72[c]
Percent of respondents who answered: Their relationships with clients are "excellent"[a]	92	89	83	87	60	86	72	87	55	82[c]
Agency wants to set a "tough tone" with clients[a]	0	16	0	12	47	0	18	7	8	11
Staff are "very likely" to go out of their way to help a client[a]	77	58	83	50	13	81	63	63	16	56

Clients view staff who monitor "much more" as helper/counselor than as rule enforcer[a]	42	33	57	8	7	23	21	20	32	25
Number of Staff Surveyed	13	19	24	26	15	36	40	30	37	240

SOURCE: MDRC Staff Activities and Attitudes Survey.

NOTE: The sample for this table includes all GAIN line staff from each county and a random subsample of eligibility workers in Fresno. The order in which the counties appear on the table is based on the number of registrants in each county's GAIN program as of December 1987. Napa had the lowest number, and Fresno had the highest.

Percentages reported in the table are based on the number of respondents who answered each question.

[a]"EW" stands for "eligibility workers."

[b]"Percentage high" on each scale represents the percent of respondents who scored above the median score on the scale.

[c]The total for this variable does not include eligibility workers in Fresno.

[d]Percentages report staff who answered "6" or "7" on a seven-point scale. The phrase in quotations indicates the endpoint of the scale.

TABLE 7.5
Staff Perceptions of the Goals of GAIN, by County

Goal of GAIN/ Respondent's Answer	Napa	San Mateo	Butte	Ventura	Kern	Stanislaus	Santa Clara	Fresno	Total
1. To get welfare clients into unsubsidized jobs:									
"Very strongly" emphasized by their agency	85%	71%	79%	44%	67%	71%	62%	57%	64%
Personally feel goal is "very important"	77	63	88	65	67	89	69	64	72
2. To reduce welfare costs for government in the long run:									
"Very strongly" emphasized by their agency	42	61	50	52	57	38	52	36	46
Personally feel goal is "very important"	54	42	58	58	73	71	40	59	57
3. To make continuous participation mandatory for nonexempt clients:									
"Very strongly" emphasized by their agency	62	61	87	83	79	65	58	40	62
Personally feel goal is "very important"	54	56	74	60	47	77	44	56	58

4. To reduce stigma and psychological burden of clients while on welfare:									
"Very strongly" emphasized by their agency	83%	50%	61%	17%	13%	49%	34%	31%	39%
Personally feel goal is "very important"	85	89	74	63	47	74	49	49	62
5. To give clients more choice about services they receive:									
"Very strongly" emphasized by their agency	77	50	58	26	40	48	45	34	44
Personally feel goal is "very important"	85	72	79	58	67	67	63	40	61
6. To improve relationship between welfare workers and clients:									
"Very strongly" emphasized by their agency	62	53	65	16	7	53	45	36	42
Personally feel goal is "very important"	75	79	83	54	33	85	58	55	64
Number of Staff Surveyed	13	19	24	26	15	36	40	67	240

SOURCE: MDRC Staff Activities and Attitudes Survey.

NOTES: The sample for this table includes all GAIN line staff from each county and a random subsample of eligibility workers in Fresno.

The order in which the counties appear on the table is based on the number of registrants in each county's GAIN program as of December 1987. Napa had the lowest number and Fresno had the highest.

Percentages reported in the table are based on the number of respondents who answered each question.

Percentages report staff who answered "6" or "7" on a seven-point scale. The phrase in quotation marks indicates the endpoint of the scale.

TABLE 7.6

Eligibility Workers' Knowledge of and Attitudes Toward GAIN, by County

Survey Item	Napa	San Mateo	Butte	Ventura	Kern	Stanislaus	Santa Clara	Fresno	Total
Knowledge of GAIN									
Percent of respondents who answered:									
EWs are "very knowledgeable" about GAIN[a,b]	19%	22%	17%	17%	15%	11%	20%	—	17%
They attended a training session about GAIN[b,c]	47	57	93	79	37	68	53	—	64
Attitudes toward GAIN:									
Percent of respondents who answered:									
"Strongly agree" that someone who wants to get off welfare can get a lot of help from workers' agency	80	25	25	34	33	29	20	34	32
Feel that GAIN services can give clients "considerable help" in getting off welfare	88	44	30	21	26	25	32	16	30
Feel that GAIN services can give clients "considerable help" in feeling better about themselves	88	44	47	21	33	36	30	24	36

Feel "strongly" that they have something positive to offer clients because of GAIN[b]	69%	75%	53%	38%	30%	41%	37%	—	44%
The eligibility worker's workload Percent of respondents who answered:									
The job of the EW has been "substantially" affected by GAIN[a,b]	67	78	24	46	31	27	25	—	36
The job of the EW has been "much" harder under GAIN[a,b]	47	67	25	39	13	42	31	—	34
GAIN has made the paperwork "much" harder[b]	47	56	33	28	36	37	32	—	35
The job of the EW has been "much" more satisfying under GAIN[a,b]	60	25	19	15	14	9	12	—	19
Sample size	16	9	30	29	34	28	41	37	224

SOURCE: MDRC Staff Activities and Attitudes Survey.

NOTES: The sample for this table includes a random subsample of eligibility workers from each county.

The order in which the counties appear on the table is based on the number of registrants in each county's GAIN program as of December 1987. Napa had the lowest number, and Fresno had the highest.

Percentages reported in the table are based on the number of respondents who answered each question.

Percentages report staff who answered "6" or "7" on a seven-point scale. The phrase in quotations indicates the endpoint of the scale.

[a] "EW" stands for "eligibility worker."

[b] Eligibility workers in Fresno and seven eligibility workers in Kern were not asked this question.

[c] Percentages for this variable report staff who answered "yes."

role, at least in theory, was supposed to resemble the new-style work-fare case management model. However, because of the high cost of using trained social workers in this way, and also because of concern over the intrusiveness of the idea of social workers "fixing up" the lives of welfare families, the federal government issued regulations early in the 1970s that separated the social work and eligibility functions. The latter functions were assigned to lower-level clerical personnel called eligibility workers. (My own view now is that this was a mistake, although I was serving in the federal government and was not of this opinion at the time.) In effect the idea of new-style workfare goes back to the earlier model of having a trained professional person in charge of each separate service, although the focus is now on employment and training as the central purpose of this relationship. The role of case managers under new-style workfare is an important indicator, at least in my view, as to whether real change is made in the mission and role of welfare bureaucracies. A number of important questions follow from this observation.

Should GAIN case managers be generalists or specialists? The generalist model is appealing, the idea being that a recipient should have a continuous relationship with a GAIN case manager and come to know and work closely with that person. The catch is that program components, as we have seen, are different and often physically dispersed. Especially in the larger counties in the MDRC-GAIN sample, these considerations led to the adoption of systems in which specialized GAIN case managers were responsible for different services, such as child care, education, job search, training, etc. Santa Clara, the county with the largest population in the sample (1,431,000), was found by MDRC researchers to have "one of the most specialized systems."[8] There were two basic GAIN program units, one for intake and another for ongoing case management. Each was housed in separate offices with its own supervisor.[9] Within these two units, responsibilities were further subdivided.

MDRC researchers found that caseload size per worker and the depth and character of services varied among the sample counties, within counties, and over time. Kern County had especially high case-loads per worker "partly reflecting the decision of GAIN administrators to stretch program resources by serving a high volume of registrants at the expense of intensive case manager involvement."[10] In Butte County (population 177,000), registrants were "routinely placed in an unassigned pool after orientation." Overall, MDRC found that "the counties were largely successful in creating service networks comprehensive enough to offer the main components required by the GAIN legislation."[11]

The MDRC-GAIN evaluation report includes consideration of the extent to which, and the way in which, recipients participated in education, training, job search activities, etc. The service activities of those who participated in a post orientation component are shown in table 7.7.

There are a number of important points in these data. Participation was higher among the voluntary than the mandatory registrants. But note that the proportion of volunteers who participated in "self-initiated" education or training was higher than for the mandatory registrants (39.1 percent versus 14.1 percent for the AFDC Family Group). This explains almost all of the difference in the participation rates between the mandatory and voluntary registrants (see line two in table 7.7) and is understandable. People already in education or training programs, even if they are not required to participate in the GAIN program, need to register in order to receive benefits related to GAIN participation, notably child care and continuing Medicaid coverage. Still, one-third of the mandatory registrants and two-thirds of the volunteers participated in education and training (line seven), although one must remember that one program-day is all that it took to be so classified. Education and training is the stand-out category among service components. This reflects the way the GAIN law was written. Testing for literacy and arithmetic skills is the initial up-front requirement, with the stipulation that people who fail these tests must be referred to education and remediation programs. The California law was pace-setting in this regard. The sequence of services under GAIN puts education in a special position as the required entry-level service for registrants who lack basic literacy and arithmetic skills. In the past, education had not even been an eligible activity under work-welfare programs. Its inclusion in GAIN had a strong influence on national policy. One of the most distinctive departures from past practices in the JOBS program under the Family Support Act was the inclusion of education as an activity for purposes of federal reimbursement under state welfare employment programs.

This aspect of the GAIN law had a big impact on the start-up of the new program. The failure rate on the entry tests was much higher than expected. It was anticipated to be around 25 percent, but was found in practice to be over twice that. The failure rate was 55 percent in a pilot

TABLE 7.7

Percent of Orientation Attenders Involved in Specified Activities Within Four Months of Orientation, by GAIN Status and Assistance Category

	Mandatory Registrants		Voluntary Registrants
Activity	AFDC-FG	AFDC-U	AFDC-FG
Participated, including self-initiated education or training[a]	47.3%	49.5%	71.2%
Participated, excluding self-initiated education or training[a]	33.4	43.4	34.2
Participated in any job search	13.7	25.0	16.7
job club	8.9	13.1	14.7
Supervised job search	4.8	11.2	2.9
90-day job search	0.7	1.6	0.0
Participated in any education or training	34.4	28.1	61.7
Self-initiated education or training[b]	14.1	6.5	39.1
Program-referred education or training	20.3	21.6	24.6
Basic education[c]	19.9	21.1	23.1
English as a second language	4.7	8.6	0.5
Adult basic education	8.5	8.3	10.1
GED preparation	6.8	4.2	12.7
Postassessment education or training	0.5	0.6	2.5
Assessed	4.3	5.7	7.6
Participated in work experience	1.2	0.7	0.2
Deferred	41.6	33.3	4.7
Referred for money management	2.6	1.4	0.0
Deregistered	18.7	28.0	36.5
Due to sanctioning	0.7	0.2	4.2
Due to other reasons	18.0	27.8	32.3
Received GED, postappraisal	1.0	1.8	7.7
Employed[d]	21.3	29.3	12.0
Sample size	611	541	276

SOURCE: Members of MDRC's participant flow sample who attended orientation within two months of registration.

NOTES: The sample for this table is weighted to reflect county caseload sizes.

Fresno is not included in these activity measures because of unavailable data.

Activity indicators include individuals who participated in a particular activity, or who were in a particular status, for at least one day during the follow-up period.

Subcategory percentages may not add to category percentages because sample members can be included in more than one activity.

[a]This includes participation in job search, education, training, and work experience activities. It does not include attendance at orientation, appraisal, assessment, GED receipt, or employment.

[b]Data are available only for the first occurrence of self-initiated education or training.

[c]Included here is program-referred basic education. Very few self-initiated registrants were active in basic education programs.

[d]"Employed" includes any indication of employment found in individuals' case files, including employment that resulted in deferral or deregistration or that occurred after an individual left welfare.

study conducted shortly after the GAIN law was passed and before it was implemented in the start-up counties. Like the pilot study, the early program experience showed higher than anticipated failure rates. Persons who failed the test did have the choice of entering an education program or going directly to job search.[12] As shown in table 7.7, job search was the second largest activity category. Because of this first-step requirement of referral to and emphasis on education, the GAIN program placed heavy demands on adult schools and community colleges.

A key question one would want to ask about the participation in GAIN activities involves duration. Was participation continuous as the law envisioned and, if not, how close was it to this standard? Earlier, I pointed out that 11 percent of the total of the mandatory registrants met a "continuous" participation standard defined as being active in a GAIN component for more than 70 percent of the days they were in the program. When the denominator is orientation attenders (rather than all mandatory registrants) the rate is higher, 41 percent for volunteers and 19.5 percent for mandatory AFDC participants, as shown in table 7.8. Is this good or bad? The answer is in the eyes of the beholder. My own reaction is that if this performance level is sustained and generalized, it is an impressive institutional achievement.

THE SANCTIONING PROCESS

What happens to people who do not participate in GAIN, either because they fail to show up for orientation and are not deferred, or because they are referred to an activity and fail to report or participate on a regular basis? The debate about the way the enforcement and penalty provisions should work was critical in the development of the program; it was basic to the political bargain necessary to win conservative support for enactment.

GAIN legislation creates a complex penalty process. The aim is to "allow counties to enforce the participation mandate but at the same time . . . protect registrants against unreasonable expectations or unfair punishment."[13] The first step for clients who do not fulfill program requirements is conciliation, both informal and formal. After conciliation, the law requires two further steps, beginning with three months of what is called "money management," an arrangement whereby a third party (usually an eligibility worker) is supposed to receive and

TABLE 7.8

Percent of Orientation Attenders, by Percent of Days Active out of Days in Active/ Available Status During the Four Months Following Orientation, by GAIN Status and Assistance Category

Percent of Days Active out of Days in Active/Available Status	Mandatory Registrants		Voluntary Registrants
	AFDC-FG	AFDC-U	AFDC-FG
Never active	46.2%	43.8%	27.4%
Ever active	53.8	56.3	72.7
At least 1 percent	53.8	56.3	72.7
At least 10 percent	50.5	49.4	68.3
At least 20 percent	42.4	41.7	61.7
At least 30 percent	36.1	34.6	57.4
At least 40 percent	31.3	28.8	53.7
At least 50 percent	27.8	25.2	47.1
At least 60 percent	22.6	21.3	42.9
At least 70 percent	19.5	17.7	41.1
At least 80 percent	17.0	14.7	31.0
At least 90 percent	11.5	10.1	24.0
100 percent	0.1	0.3	0.0
Sample size	507	463	264

SOURCE: Members of MDRC's participant flow sample who attended orientation within two months of registration.

NOTES: The sample for this table is weighted to reflect county caseload sizes.

Fresno is not included in these calculations because of unavailable data.

"Days active" represents all days in which the individual was enrolled in job search, education, training, work experience, or assessment, starting with the first day of participation and ending with the activity interruption or end date (including weekends). It does not include orientation, appraisal, GED receipt or employment.

"Days Active" was calculated by summing all days enrolled in an activity. Sample members with missing status start dates, or with missing activity start or end dates, are not included in this table. Therefore sample sizes are smaller than on other tables that present results for orientation attenders.

"Active/available status" represents all days during the follow-up period in which the individual was judged by program staff to be available to be assigned to a program activity.

All percentage calculations are based on all registrants noted in the "Sample size" row.

make payments from the welfare grant. The final step in the penalty process is grant reduction or termination. In the case of single-parent families, the reduction equals the grant amount for the family head for three months initially and for six months for a second offense. In the case of two-parent welfare families, the entire welfare grant is terminated for the first transgression.

Table 7.7 shows that 2.6 percent of the AFDC family group registrants and 1.4 percent of the intact families were referred to money management. No volunteers were referred. However, more people in the volunteer group (4.2 percent) were deregistered due to sanctioning than in the two mandatory participation groups where the percentages for this outcome are tiny.

The largest category for persons who are deregistered, as shown in table 7.7, is "for other reasons." For the most part, this involves personal reasons, such as having another child, illness, etc. (The data from counties are limited, so we do not know the specific reasons for these actions.) The relatively small number of people shown as deregistered due to sanctioning may be a function of the time it takes to reach this point in the process; the MDRC observation period for some cases may not have been long enough to capture what was happening in this respect. MDRC staff stated that additional sanctioning actions appeared to be occurring that could not be captured in the time period for this research.[14] The relatively small amount of deregistration due to sanctioning is a function in some counties of an emphasis on the part of GAIN workers on "persuasion" as opposed to an "enforcement" approach to program management.

In MDRC's first implementation report, one of the main problems described was "no-shows" at the front end of the GAIN process, that is, people scheduled for orientation sessions who did not show up. This had not been anticipated. It required county officials to devise procedures to locate and contact no-shows. The second MDRC implementation report quotes one county administrator saying, "Everyone was so focused on what a wonderful opportunity this was for clients that no one considered the possibility they might resist participating."[15] Counties in the sample for the second MDRC-GAIN implementation report varied in the way they dealt with the no-show problem. Napa and Santa Clara counties, for example, created specialist positions to enforce orientation attendance.[16] Other counties relied on informal approaches. Some used home visits; others did not.

Overall, the MDRC report suggests a high level of worker sympathy with clients. However, this assessment is balanced by comments showing that GAIN staff had doubts about clients' statements about barriers to participation. Excerpts from the report demonstrate an ambivalence on this score among welfare workers. On the one hand:

> GAIN staff consistently engaged in a variety of responses to lax attendance—from offering encouragement and problem solving to sending warning letters—before invoking money management and sanctions, as prescribed in the GAIN legislation. In fact, in the field interviews the GAIN staff generally expressed sympathy for registrants' problems with

child care, illness, family relationships, and other circumstances that caused them to miss program activities. Their sympathy may have been engendered in part by their own general views on the causes of poverty and welfare dependency, which tended to give situational explanations prominence.

On the other hand:

> Nonetheless, the GAIN staff did not always interpret registrants' problems as sufficient excuses for poor attendance in GAIN activities. In response to a staff survey item asking how many registrants they believed were "overstating their barriers to participating in the GAIN program," only 24 percent of the staff said "very few." Most (63 percent) gave answers falling in the middle range of the scale, indicating that they believed a considerable number of registrants were overstating their obstacles to participation.[17]

The element in the penalty process that the field researchers found to be especially cumbersome was money management. One GAIN case manager was quoted as saying that some clients liked the idea of money management: "Some of my clients ask to be put on money management. They say, 'As long as it pays my bills, that's great.' I don't think it's a deterrent."[18] Among the few recommendations made by the MDRC in the second GAIN implementation report was one to abolish this step in the penalty process on the grounds that money management "did not appear to encourage participation and was difficult to administer."[19] This was done.

CONCLUDING COMMENT

This close and detailed look at the local operations of GAIN, based on the MDRC research, helps us a great deal. It does not however allow precise numeric observations about the degree of institutional change that has taken place, though it reveals a lot more than would otherwise be known about what is involved in attempting to accomplish this change. Even when more data are available, I am sure there will be room for observers to draw different conclusions about the efficacy of new-style workfare, depending on their beliefs about the policy being advanced and their expectations about the amount, kinds, and rate of institutional change that can be achieved. I see the policy leaders (legislative and administrative) in California as having achieved appreciable institutional change. I have to admit, however, that I have two biases: I am in sympathy with the concept of new-style workfare as embodied in the GAIN program, and I have a healthy respect for the magnitude of the institutional challenge involved in implementing it. It appears that both top-down and bottom-up processes are at work in California. Some counties, although small, provide a political setting conducive to GAIN, whereas leaders in other counties appear to be resistant. In sum, institutional change seems to be occurring, although it is uneven. However, the policy environment on contoversial social issues is invariably and frequently fluid. As this book goes to press there are signs of a pullback on the implementation of GAIN due to the state's tightening fiscal crisis and an increasingly hard-edged mood on welfare issues.

CHAPTER

8

Feedback and Program Oversight

I t is common to assume that heads of large public agencies will seek feedback from the field to increase their managerial effectiveness. But, alas, the world may not work this way. Political scientist Herbert Kaufman conducted an ingenious study in the 1970s to test the proposition that managers want to know what is going on in their agency. Kaufman studied the flow of data about subordinate behavior into the headquarters of nine federal government bureaus. Although he did his work before computers had been developed for the rapid transmission of field data, Kaufman found that while the leaders of the bureaus he studied did have the capacity to keep track of what was going on below them, they often did not bother to do so. In fact, many bureau leaders, said Kaufman, "may prefer *not* to seek irrefutable evidence of the whole truth." [1] They may not want to know about things they cannot fix or that "they privately approve of . . . that they know they should, according to law and morality, prevent." [2] This is not to argue against management oversight, but rather to set the scene by being skeptical as to whether it is always and automatically done and desired. In this chapter, I consider the ways the managers of new-style workfare programs did, or did not, set up systems for feedback and obtain and use information from the field.

There are several types of information about program operations that can be used as feedback to headquarters to gauge management effectiveness. One is internal agency information. Another is information from external sources, which managers often do not receive with delight and eagerness. Major sources of external feedback are the press, other bureaus of government, the legislature, and in some cases the courts, as well as reports from interest groups that have a stake in the business at hand. A third type of feedback is more formal evaluation research. The implementation study of the California GAIN program conducted by the Manpower Demonstration Research Corporation (MDRC), described in the previous chapter, is a case in point. For a number of reasons, Massachusetts offers an interesting case for all three types of feedback—internal, external, and evaluation research. The Massachusetts experience is stressed, though not used exclusively, in this chapter.

INTERNAL FEEDBACK

The management strategy of the top administrators of the ET program in Massachusetts featured close monitoring of program data related to central purposes of the program. The commissioner of public welfare, Charles Atkins, and his deputy, Thomas Glynn, made a major point of setting, changing, and tracking highly visible numerical goals for the ET program. This is one of Atkins's managerial trademarks. His magic number is ten; as commissioner, he developed and stuck to a system of issuing and monitoring ten goals that were changed annually.

Robert D. Behn, in his management study of the ET Choices program, observed that if Atkins were to resign as commissioner (which he did in 1989), "the first thing his successor would be asked is: 'What are your ten goals?' "[3] (In fact, his successor told me in an interview shortly after Atkins left office that she would keep the ten-goal system.) Atkins's goals shifted each year and involved setting targets both for local offices and individual workers. Goals were publicized widely and disseminated to all employees; they were subdivided by local office and within the local offices by program unit. Regular status reports were widely disseminated. There was no escaping the eagle eye of ET.

In May 1983, when Atkins became commissioner, the number one goal was to reduce the state's AFDC error rate, which then stood at

11.4 percent, the third highest in the nation.[4] The goal was to reduce the error rate to 9 percent; the goal for 1984 was 5 percent. Over the years, as the department succeeded in reducing the AFDC error rate (it was eventually reduced below the 3 percent level at which federal sanctions are supposed to be triggered), this goal dropped in rank in the list of ten goals.

The number two goal in Atkins's first year as commissioner was 6,000 job placements under ET. This goal was increased and adjusted in future years so that, for example, in 1987 it was 10,000 job placements of which 6,000 were to be jobs that paid at least five dollars per hour after thirty days.[5] This subgoal for so-called priority placements at over five dollars per hour was described by Deputy Commissioner Glynn as "ET-II." The management team adopted a new slogan, "ET Springs Forward." [6] The five-dollar hourly threshold for priority placements was raised to six dollars the next year.

Each month the performance of the fifty-six local offices in relation to their ET job-placement goal was logged and closely assessed. Initially, many local offices (half at the end of six months) were below their quota, and Atkins and his management team let them know about it. According to Behn, "as the people who worked for the department—particularly the directors of the local offices—began to realize that the goals were serious, performance continued to improve." [7] Prodding and praise were constant and highly visible. At the end of the second year of ET, Governor Dukakis presented awards to the thirty-seven out of fifty-six local offices that had achieved their ET job-placement goal. On this occasion, the governor said the ET program is "the most exciting new program in the nation . . . no department in state government should be prouder of its track record over the last eighteen months. Again and again I have turned to you. Again and again you have delivered." [8]

As the ET goals were ratcheted up, so was the managerial rhetoric. A year later at the department's annual conference, the governor told departmental employees "the progress that has been made in your department is phenomenal." In 1986, the ET job-placement goal was exceeded by 25 percent, and for the first time all of the local offices were above target.[9] One has to be impressed by this skillful use of "significant numbers," with targets set and adjusted on a basis that both sustained momentum and gave the impression within and outside of the agency of going "over the top" in the campaign to implement ET.

The message was clear. What was desired was to place ET participants in good jobs that would enable them to get off of welfare. True, the program was voluntary, but the "newspeak" of welfare in Massachusetts about self-sufficiency and reducing the rolls was so pronounced that, as pointed out in earlier chapters, the line between encouraging and pushing people to enter ET became finer and finer.

According to Behn's analysis, this ratcheted-up goal-setting process, while flexible from year to year, was one of the keys to the agency's success. Behn likened this process to that in the private sector. In *In Search of Excellence,* Peters and Waterman said high-performance private companies "are full of hoopla . . . . They actively seek out and pursue endless excuses to give out awards." [10] Endorsing the Atkins approach, Behn says, "Without specific goals, the most inspiring statement of purposes has little meaning." [11]

Behn's judgment and that of other observers is that the Atkins system did permeate the agency, affecting the behavior of workers, the signals they transmitted, and the services they provided to welfare family heads. But all was not peaches and cream for ET. Some outside observers found fault, criticizing the hype and hoopla and questioning the veracity of the claims made by Governor Dukakis and Atkins and his management team.

Before examining these criticisms it is useful to consider data systems for other states in the sample. Michigan stands out for having good data issued regularly, although, as I have noted earlier, its management strategy for the MOST program was decidedly low-key compared to Massachusetts. Both states have state-administered welfare systems.

Of the two states in the sample that have state-supervised, county-administered welfare systems (California and New Jersey), New Jersey has by far the better data system, though the state did not use a goal-setting and monitoring strategy comparable in intensity and hype to that of Massachusetts. The New Jersey OMEGA data system for tracking REACH participants is a model system. In contrast, California still does not have a centralized data system for the GAIN program, a subject that has been controversial in state government for a long time. Overall, the state's management style for GAIN is much looser and more decentralized than that of the other case-study states. This may be a reflection of the tradition of welfare programs in California and also of the scale of the task involved in setting up a centralized welfare data system in a state the size of California, and particularly in its largest county Los Angeles.

EXTERNAL FEEDBACK

In the three case-study states in which the welfare employment program was most visible (Massachusetts, California, and New Jersey), the press frequently covered controversies about these policies. The liveliest controversies in the media occurred in Massachusetts. Leading the charge was Warren T. Brookes, formerly a reporter for the *Boston Globe*, who later joined the Washington bureau of the *Detroit News*. Brookes crusaded against ET. He wrote sharply critical articles about the program, centering his one-man vendetta against the program on its voluntary character. An able investigative reporter with good analytical skills, Brookes's articles raised questions that go to the heart of new-style workfare.

In a 1987 article in the *Wall Street Journal,* Brookes charged, "The results in Massachusetts are so poor as to call into question the entire ET program as a waste of taxpayer dollars, now nearly $50 million a year." [12] Brookes compared the Massachusetts record with that in neighboring New Hampshire to argue that considering the booming economy in New England in the early 1980s, the people who exited welfare for jobs would have done so anyway. Citing the less expensive effort in New Hampshire, he said the record there in reducing the welfare rolls was better and the costs lower. Massachusetts, according to Brookes, spent sixteen times more per client on its welfare training and outreach program than New Hampshire and experienced relatively much smaller caseload reductions. In the three years from 1983 to 1986, the Massachusetts caseload rose by one-half a percentage point, said Brookes, whereas the rolls declined by 30 percent in this same period in New Hampshire. Michigan, too, according to Brookes, had a better record than Massachusetts:

> Indeed, given its much greater challenge, Michigan has much more to show for its $50 million annual MOST program, with compulsory job training and placement. During the same three year period as above [September 1983 to September 1986] it cut its basic AFDC caseloads 5 percent, and new AFDC applications fell about 15 percent and 27 percent respectively, for a lower-cost (for relative caseload) program that apparently is working in a state with a relatively high (8 percent) unemployment level. [13]

Brookes's strongest attacks on ET appeared in the *Washington Times,* a newspaper that is often a forum for conservative views on social issues. Brookes also directed his fire at the emerging national welfare legislation in the Congress. In a number of articles in the *Washington Times,* Brookes used his ammunition on ET to attack different versions of what ultimately became the Family Support Act of 1988. He was most outspoken in his opposition to the House-passed bill.

In December 1987 Brookes noted in an article in the *Washington Times* that House Democrats were being forced to cut back the bill they were pressing because of its cost and also "because it is tailored after a Massachusetts program, known as ET, which has done a lot for the state's welfare bureaucracy—but little to cut welfare caseloads." [14] Repeating arguments against such programs that he had made before, Brookes cited the rise in AFDC caseloads in Massachusetts in a period in which caseloads were falling in other states, and which, he charged, was occurring despite the state's increasing employment. Brookes said, "welfare costs have soared" in Massachusetts: "From 1983 to 1988, welfare administration costs (not counting ET) have risen from $74.2 million to $114 million, a monstrous 53.6 percent rise, or, after inflation, a huge 30 percent real increase." Adding the coup de grace, Brookes said, "At the same time, ET direct costs, including day care vouchers, have skyrocketed from $6.9 million in FY '83 to $59.2 million in FY '88. The cost per welfare job placement has soared from $1,360 in FY '83 to more than $6,000 in 1987." [15]

In this article, Brookes also cited approvingly a Heritage Foundation book by Stuart Butler and Anna Kondratas that he said revealed the pitfalls of the Massachusetts approach. Interestingly, the Butler-Kondratas book, while noting that the cost-saving potential for work-welfare should not be overstated, supported the basic approach of reciprocal obligations under the new-style workfare:

> So, although the case for workfare is usually made on cost-saving and dependency-reducing grounds, there is no clear evidence that any savings will in fact be forthcoming in the short run. Depending on the design and goals of the program, it can be either more or less expensive than welfare without work requirements. Nevertheless, it is important for society to send a clear message, and workfare sends it: Good welfare policy must involve reciprocal obligations. [16]

Several issues are raised by the attacks on the ET program. One is ideological. Brookes, like other conservatives who write about these issues, saw the ET program as likely to draw people to the welfare rolls because it provided additional benefits. The opportunity to receive relatively generous educational and child care benefits, and the provisions for transitional aid (medical and child care) when recipients enter the labor force, is seen by conservatives as making welfare more attractive. For many liberals, on the other hand, this outreach and service-provision role, far from being a flaw in the design, is viewed as one of its great strengths.

Conservatives bridled at Dukakis's conception of welfare employment programs, especially his insistence that they should be voluntary. This is ironic, since I have pointed out earlier that in operation at ground level the ET program placed more pressure on welfare family heads than any of the other programs I studied. Nevertheless, as argued by Butler and Kondratas and generally agreed to by conservative experts on social policy, welfare employment programs (if there are to be such programs at all) must be mandatory in order to convey a strong prowork signal and to deter people from coming on and staying on the welfare rolls.

A more sophisticated issue raised by conservative critics such as Brookes involves what social science researchers call the *counterfactual*. The term refers to what would have happened anyway, that is, in this case without the existence of the ET program. Brookes, as I have noted, stressed the Massachusetts economic boom as the reason people left the rolls. He said, "More than half of the monthly case terminations were people finding jobs on their own," and added, "All of this was in an economy whose basic unemployment rate fell more than 40 percent from 7.2 percent in September 1983 to 4.2 percent in last September 1986." [17] Other newspaper articles raised the same issue of the counterfactual state. *Fortune* magazine ran a story in October 1985 that reflected this Brookes line. Although it was more positive about the idea of new-style workfare, the article questioned the claims made for these programs, in particular the Massachusetts program. The story stated that "Massachusetts has not compared the ET graduates with a control group and is claiming savings from thousands of employed welfare recipients who probably would have found jobs anyway. The numbers that state officials like to toss around also tend to distort the program's success, since only 31 percent of welfare recipients participated in ET." The *Fortune* story then went on to temper this criticism, pointing out that "the income levels of ET graduates really are impressive. Those who found full-time jobs during the first half of the year received an average annual starting salary of $12,000 vs. an average annual AFDC grant of about $5,000." [18]

In brief, the criticisms of welfare employment programs in the press depicted those programs as costing too much, not having a real impact (people would have gotten jobs anyway), and attracting people to come on or stay on welfare because of the availability of new services and benefits.

Despite these issues and the efforts of conservative critics to press them, most of the press feedback for ET in Massachusetts was positive. Favorable press accounts stressed examples of people who were aided by the new programs in dramatic ways. In February 1987, *Newsweek* wrote a story about ET headlined, "Welfare: A New Drive to Clean Up the Mess, A Broad-Based Attack on a Pathological Problem." The *Newsweek* story said that Governor Michael Dukakis's "reputation as a 1988 presidential candidate has been buoyed by ET's success." [19] Writing in the *New York Times,* John Herbers, who visited ET sites, wrote a similarly positive account.

> The program's upbeat message is evident in Dorchester, a poor neighborhood in Boston, where the welfare office has been moved from a dingy, cramped building to a restored spacious old Roman Catholic school. Every morning, the arriving poor—in this neighborhood mostly Hispanic people and some blacks—are greeted with a sales pitch about work even before the applicants are assigned to caseworkers.
>
> The walls are decorated with color posters, including ones made to look like a Monopoly game with "day care vouchers" and "transportation allowances" as chance cards and a career opening as the payoff for passing "Go." Cookies and coffee are free.[20]

Prior to the *Newsweek* and *Times* stories, the *Washington Post* ran an article in February 1987 making no bones about its view. The headline said, "New Welfare Strategy Works in Massachusetts, Bay State Lauds Its Job-Incentive Program." The *Post* story stressed the voluntary nature of the Massachusetts program as "snubbing workfare." Like many such stories, it featured a successful participant, in this case Judy Boyd, divorced, aged twenty-five, a trainee to be a hospital surgery assistant. " 'I'm hoping one day to buy a home,' Boyd said, pausing to savor the thought, then giggling with pride and excitement." [21] the *Wall Street Journal* in a front page story gave a less ebullient but still upbeat account of ET.[22] Good press feedback far exceeded the bad.

Other reactions came from government agencies and outside organizations. The Massachusetts Taxpayers Foundation, a group that generally takes conservative positions, issued a study in August 1987 giving the ET program a clean bill of health. Although the statistical methods used in this study leave much to be desired, the report concluded that the program saved money for the taxpayers. Massachusetts received a well-publicized national award for its ET program from the Innovations in State and Local Government program, jointly sponsored by the Ford Foundation and the John F. Kennedy School of Harvard University.

FORMAL EVALUATIONS

The criticism by Warren Brookes and others of the Massachusetts ET program raises an important question for program managers about their use of, and support for, more formal evaluation studies. This is the third major type of program feedback considered in this chapter. By evaluation studies, I refer to longer and more systematic examinations of public programs as compared to more general and cursory articles in the press. Presumably the benefits of formal evaluations are that they enable managers to spot and deal with problems and, assuming a good result, they provide independent evidence of program efficacy that can be used to clear the air in debates about program effects such as the debate about the ET program.

The downside for evaluation research involves its cost, the time required to get results, and the always-present risk that the results will not confirm claims of program effectiveness. Politicians often exaggerate the benefits of the new policies they are promoting and the speed at which results will be achieved. They often feel they have to do this to win enactment of a new program, especially one focused on the poor, who have little clout or leverage.

The "Catch 22" about the use of evaluation research is that such studies frequently produce results that, while positive, fall short of the claimed benefits for "bold" new policies. We saw this in chapter 4, for example, in discussing the MDRC work-welfare studies in eleven states, which showed consistent, positive, and significant—but not large— impacts. It may be for this reason that conservatives such as Charles Hobbs in the Reagan White House argued for additional evaluation research, particularly formal evaluation studies using random assignment methods to select and compare treatment and control groups, although one must be very careful about imputing motives in these situations.[23]

In an ideal world, a welfare program manager could be expected to ask three main types of questions that evaluation researchers could answer: Was our new program put into place the way it was supposed to be (*implementation*)? Did it work, that is, did it provide benefits to recipients (*impact*)? And finally, did the costs outweigh the benefits (*cost-benefit*)?

The Massachusetts experience is again especially interesting—this time on the question of whether or not to have an evaluation done of the ET program. Initially chief policymakers and managers of the Massachusetts ET program (Governor Dukakis included) chose not to sponsor an evaluation of the program, although they were urged to do so by university, MDRC, and other outside experts. This decision contrasts with those of other state governments in the sample. In California, New Jersey, and Arkansas, evaluation studies were conducted as part of the work-welfare evaluation of the Manpower Demonstration Research Corporation. Michigan conducted its own in-house impact study. Later, Massachusetts policymakers appeared to pay a price for their decision. Members of the opposition in the legislature made charges similar to those by Warren Brookes, which in turn found their way into the presidential campaign where the credibility of the ET program was questioned. This controversy ultimately resulted in a decision to sponsor an evaluation of the ET program. The state asked research organizations to submit proposals for an evaluation. But even at this point there was some foot dragging.

The consensus among policy researchers is that the best way to measure the impact of programs on individual participants is to use random assignment. But because the ET program was supposed to be available to everyone who volunteered, state officials bridled, not without justification, at the idea that some people would have to be assigned to a control (no-treatment) group in order to conduct this most rigorous type of impact study. Citing the fact that anyone who wants to can volunteer, the Request for Proposals for evaluating ET said "methodologies involving random assignment of clients to a control group and various treatment groups would deny the client choice on which this program is based." [24] The Request for Proposals made no bones about the state's position on this issue: "The department of public welfare thus considers random assignment to be diametrically opposed to the basic philosophy of the ET Choices program." [25]

A number of research firms responded to the Massachusetts call for research proposals, and the state chose the Urban Institute to conduct the study. The Urban Institute issued its first report in November 1989 with preliminary findings on the experience of recipients who participated in ET and found jobs. The research sample contained 14,000 persons active in AFDC or ET from June 1, 1986, to June 30, 1987. The emphasis of the first report, however, was on the importance of child care and extended medical care for a job-finding subsample of 1,183 persons. The Urban Institute researchers found a positive relationship between child care and employer-provided health insurance and job retention. These findings were highlighted as "directly relevant for the implementation of the national Job Opportunities and Basic Skills (JOBS) program."[26]

On the whole, the evaluation of ET was not a good experience. Reports were delayed. Key questions were put off. Relations between state officials and researchers were strained. Fortunately for researchers as a whole, other states in the sample had better experiences with evaluation studies. In the end, all of the states were involved in some way in the use of evaluation research to test new welfare employment approaches. In addition to having been involved in the MDRC eleven-state work-welfare demonstration research, New Jersey sponsored a special outside evaluation of the REACH program. The state was actually required to do this under the terms of its waiver agreement with the federal government, although this study, like the Massachusetts study, did not use a random-selection research design. In the case of Michigan, researchers for the state's Department of Social Services studied a sample of six thousand MOST registrants, some of whom were randomly assigned to a control group that did not receive services. There were about two thousand persons in both the treatment and control groups. Very similar to MDRC's findings, the results showed some, but not large, gains in earnings and income for MOST participants. They also showed significant differences in time worked and the ability of clients to hold and retain jobs. This finding, said the research report, is important and "is corroborated by other research in the field. . . . In particular an MDRC evaluation of the CWEP program in San Diego reported similar employment rate results as did an MDRC evaluation project in Maryland."[27]

CONCLUDING COMMENTS

It is tempting for a social scientist to end this chapter in the usual way with a discussion of the need for further research. Clearly, however, the most important feedback mechanism for this analysis of the implementation process involves the use of program data by state policy officials to monitor their various brands of new-style workfare. In fact, evaluation research by social scientists has a mixed record, although the experience with new-style workfare—notably, the influence of the MDRC studies on the enactment of the Family Support Act of 1988— stands out as a success story. I believe there is an important role for applied social science, not only in the design of social policy but in its implementation. The next chapter recounts the initial research findings from the ten-state implementation study of the JOBS program under the Family Support Act of 1988.

9

Implementing the JOBS Program

The Family Support Act of 1988, hailed as a new consensus between liberals and conservatives and the most sweeping revision of the nation's welfare system in the past fifty years, contains a note of irony. I worry that future historians may say that after the new law was signed, at least initially, the nation did less—rather than more—to advance its purposes. The 1988 law, as we have seen, was grounded in the efforts of the leading states that advanced new-style workfare under amendments to the 1981 Budget Act. A number of states, among them Massachusetts, California, and New Jersey, took important initiatives under the 1981 budget amendments, and studies by the Manpower Demonstration Research Corporation showed that these initiatives had good results. There is a nice logic to this sequence of events. The ideas embodied in "demonstration" programs under the 1981 law were refined in the cauldron of experience, tested by researchers, and certified as effective. They were then to be replicated throughout the country under a new federal law making this a national program. There seemed to be a truce in the welfare war in 1988. The political seas were calm.

Everything was in place. Maybe this time we would fulfill the often-inflated expectations about the start-up of a new law, in this case signed with a flourish by President Reagan in the White House Rose Garden in October 1988.

But unfortunately the picture gets blurred after all the hoopla. The story of implementing JOBS—at least so far—is not all that upbeat. The programs of some of the states that were leaders under the 1981 amendments lost steam after 1988 and the states that were new to the field entered it cautiously. The prospects for implementation are not bright as of mid-1992, although we do not at this time have enough information to draw firm conclusions.

The discussion in this chapter is based on the state-level findings from the first phase of the ten-state study of the implementation of the JOBS program. The research is part of a longer-term study that will eventually include two rounds of field research in ten states and thirty local sites in these states, including worker and client surveys at the local sites. The evaluation is being conducted by a network of field researchers based at the Nelson A. Rockefeller Institute of Government, the public policy research arm of the State University of New York, located in Albany. The study is directed by Jan L. Hagen and Irene Lurie. Their first report, *Implementing Jobs: Initial State Choices,* was issued in March 1992. It is based on observations made between October and December 1990, by which time five of the ten states in the sample had one year or more of operations under federally approved JOBS programs. The ten states in the sample are: Georgia, Maryland, Michigan, Minnesota, Mississippi, New York, Oklahoma, Oregon, Pennsylvania, and Texas.

The Hagen-Lurie study is organized to track the major features of the JOBS program. Overall, the authors saw some progress being made, but cautioned that it is still early. Nonetheless, they concluded "from our review of the initial phase of JOBS implementation that states have come closer to meeting the letter of the law than the spirit of the law." [1]

> For the most part, the hope that states would use JOBS implementation as an opportunity to signal a change in the mission of welfare systems or to redefine the social contract has not been realized. In none of the study states did JOBS spur state leaders to alter their public stance toward welfare or to make a strong personal commitment to reform their welfare programs in light of the new law. The creative and enthusiastic response

of Massachusetts and several other states to the optional WIN Demonstration and Title IV-A work programs was not replicated by the implementation of JOBS in the ten states examined here.[2]

The funny things that happened on the way to the forum for JOBS implementation are well known in the field. First and foremost, rising state budget pressures and the national recession placed fiscal strain on state governments at precisely the time the JOBS program called for additional spending to match the new money provided under the Family Support Act. Pressures were also caused by federal mandates, particularly rising demands under Medicaid, the fastest-growing and largest of all federal grant-in-aid programs, for health care services and nursing-home care. Similar pressures for prison construction strained state finances in this period.

Another factor slowing the JOBS bandwagon was that just as the paint was fresh the politics of welfare shifted. As the presidential season got under way in earnest in 1991, welfare issues took on a harsher cast, leading to budget cuts at the state and local levels that fell disproportionately on the poor.[3] These budget cuts, plus what has been called the "new paternalism" of tightened behavioral requirements associated with welfare (discussed in chapter 1), shifted the rhetoric of welfare to the right—from *services* to get people off the welfare rolls to *a general distaste* for the people on the rolls. In this climate, governors and policy leaders in the states had less incentive to push new-style workfare. Some of the zip seemed to go out of the JOBS program for these reasons, even allowing for the fact that implementing a new national policy such as JOBS in order to change bureaucratic behavior must be seen as an immensely difficult challenge, bound to take time to accomplish. Hagen and Lurie noted this kind of a zipless start-up for JOBS.

In contrast to the dramatic introduction of the JOBS program on the federal level, elected and appointed leaders in the study states introduced JOBS with relatively little fanfare. The low profile given to JOBS implementation at the state level stems from the fact that many of the states in the sample had welfare-to-work programs prior to JOBS and had already charted a course in keeping with the objectives of the federal legislation. The low-profile introduction of JOBS was also fostered by the revenue shortfalls faced by many states and by states having already established other initiatives, such as education, as state priorities.[4]

Fiscally, the JOBS program was not an unmixed blessing for the states. The federal government primed the pump but called on states to push the pump handle by having to match each new federal dollar devoted to the services provided under JOBS. The law is complicated on this score. The matching requirement is lower for poor states and for some services—for example, for child care as compared with education, training, transportation, job counseling, and assessment. For the latter services, most states need to put up forty cents for each additional dollar of federal aid they receive. While spending under JOBS increased according to Hagen and Lurie, it fell short of the amount authorized, despite the fact that the original authorization level was not lavish by federal standards. Overall, less than half of the available new JOBS funds (one billion dollars in the first year) were taken up. While the following excerpt from the Hagen-Lurie report is long, it is worth reprinting here.

> States are making widely varying efforts to fund JOBS. The majority are spending considerably more on JOBS than on previous welfare employment programs. Oregon plans to spend enough, or almost enough, to draw down its full allocation of federal funds, while Mississippi and Tennessee have appropriated very limited additional revenues for JOBS services. Administrators in half the states attributed their states' decisions to limit expenditures to constrained fiscal conditions. Funding may also have been restricted for JOBS by the need to comply with mandates of the Family Support Act to provide AFDC-UP benefits, child care, and transitional benefits.
>
> Based on the states' projections of their JOBS expenditures and preliminary information for federal fiscal year 1991, states can be divided into four groups. Low expenditure states—Mississippi and Tennessee— are drawing down less than 15 percent of their federal entitlement of JOBS funds. A middle group—Michigan, New York, Pennsylvania, and Texas—are spending enough to draw down 35 to 50 percent of their federal entitlement. Maryland, Minnesota, and Oklahoma are receiving between 55 and 70 percent of their potential funds, and Oregon is expected to draw down almost all of its federal entitlement.
>
> Expenditures in the ten study states are on average slightly lower than those in the rest of the country, although some study states are considerably above average. The ten states together drew down 43 percent of their entitlement of federal funds for 1991. Nationally, states claimed 48 percent of the federal funds allotted for this period. These levels of expenditures are a disappointment for those who expected the states to respond with the enthusiasm for JOBS expressed by its supporters at the time of enactment. Although these funding levels give only a partial

picture of the extent of services for JOBS participants because states are drawing on other resources such as the JTPA and educational services to implement JOBS, "access to services is guaranteed only by JOBS financing," as one administrator noted. If welfare agencies can be certain of obtaining services for their clients only when they have funds to purchase services, the lack of state funding for JOBS is a source of concern.[5]

Another interesting set of questions for the implementation of JOBS concerns the tone of the program. The delicate political bargain made in Washington—the *stick* of the work and participation requirements and the *carrot* of new dollars—is not easily or automatically translatable at the ground level. The founders of the new movement hoped for a push-and-pull effect—push people to participate and then pull them along with services. We saw earlier that the push (the stick) factor is not to the liking of the people who have to carry out the new policy. Indeed, Hagen and Lurie found that state policymakers preferred the "voluntary" approach. Services were the favored signal—services rather than sanctions. To quote Hagen and Lurie once more:

> Although participation is nominally mandatory for all nonexempt recipients under the Family Support Act, resource limitations have led states to set policies that make participation voluntary for many of them. Tennessee and, with a few exceptions, Minnesota have an official policy of limiting enrollment in JOBS to volunteers. The majority of the other states give high priority to volunteers or to volunteers within the target groups. At this stage in program implementation, administrators do not view the threat of sanctions as a major strategy for encouraging program participation.
>
> Most states have developed policies that give volunteers high priority for participation in JOBS. Tennessee has a formal policy, for one year only, of limiting enrollment to those who volunteer for the program. Although there are exceptions, Minnesota also has a formal policy emphasizing services to volunteers. Participation is nominally mandatory in other states, but volunteers are given priority for service. In Michigan and Pennsylvania, most participants are in practice volunteers. Mississippi and New York give priority to volunteers, while Maryland, Oklahoma, and Texas give priority to volunteers but take into account target group status as well. Only in Oregon are volunteers not given the highest priority for service.[6]

One lesson of the early experience of JOBS ties back into my previous discussion of the GAIN program in California. As I noted there, the Rube Goldberg, highly specific design of the GAIN program caused major problems for implementation. By contrast, Hagen and Lurie found that the states under JOBS chose a flexible assessment-based design rather than a rigid sequence of services.

> In general, states have chosen an assessment-based design that does not specify a fixed sequence of services or emphasize one particular service over another. The sequence and choice of services is based on each participant's assessed abilities and needs. An exception is that some states refer job-ready participants to a particular set of employment services without a full assessment.[7]

All the states in the sample were found to provide the employment-related services required by law, plus job search and on-the-job training. Community work experience, which was a source of controversy in the design of new-style workfare programs in the eighties, did not emerge as either a major service or a major issue during the early going in the Hagen-Lurie study.

As for funding, many of the studied states drew resources from other programs to supplement their JOBS activities. The most common sources of supplementary funds were the federally financed Jobs Training Partnership Act (JTPA) program, other training programs, and community colleges. These joint financial relationships make it hard to account accurately for JOBS spending. Some states (notably Mississippi, Texas, and Tennessee in the sample) relied extensively on funds from these and other programs, putting up little money from their own sources.

The major implementation issues raised by this new federal law involved the requirement that participants in JOBS spend twenty hours per week in the program, the reporting system, and the gradually stepped-up participation requirements. The twenty-hour rule was the most controversial of these issues. However, taken together these issues did not produce serious problems in the initial period studied by Hagen and Lurie.

> In the period of this study, all of the study states expected to meet both the participation rates and the targeting requirements for federal fiscal year 1991. The targeting requirements are not a major issue for any state, probably because the nonexempt caseloads are heavily composed of target group members. Responding to the seven percent participation rate requirement did not require any major programmatic changes for states in this study with relatively well developed welfare-to-work programs. However, the 20-hour rule has been of some concern in terms of

the match between the requirement to schedule 20 hours of participation and the availability of existing education and training programs, as well as the accounting mechanisms necessary to average and to track the scheduled hours of participation. It is particularly noteworthy that, by itself, full-time enrollment in a two- or four-year college program does not meet the 20-hour rule for JOBS participation.[8]

On the upside, Hagen and Lurie found that the JOBS program has potential (some of which was being realized) to bring about better linkages of services for needy families. This is an important purpose of the act and a major interest of domestic policymakers. The premise here is that important gains for poor families depend upon intervening in *whole* lives, not just single program areas. Case managers for the JOBS program were seen as playing a role in making these connections. "From the perspective of the states the federal legislation encouraged or reinforced the development of interagency coordination. . . . State agencies are drawing upon the expertise of other agencies to build the capacity to deliver JOBS services and child care."[9]

In its emphasis on education, the JOBS program breaks new ground. This was noted as a major plus in the Hagen-Lurie study. Another encouraging early finding of the Hagen-Lurie study, which accords with what MDRC and other groups had previously noted, is that child care, often described as a barrier to achieving the goals of new-style workfare, did not have this effect in the early days of implementation.

> At the time of the study, state administrators did not expect the availability of child care services or funding to affect the states' abilities to achieve the federally mandated participation rates of 7 percent for 1990 and 1991. However, the lack of sufficient child care funds has already required, or may require in the future, limiting access to the JOBS programs. Tennessee and Texas recognize the potential need to restrict program access in the future because of insufficient child care funding. To control child care costs in its program, Minnesota restricted access to JOBS in May 1990 by narrowing the groups eligible for service.[10]

LOOKING AHEAD

We owe it to supporters of JOBS (I include myself in this group) to withhold judgment. The law has great potential. But this potential can only be realized if leadership by talented agency managers at the state and local levels is devoted to changing the signals and services and the beliefs and behavior of the thousands of workers in welfare and related agencies who have to be part of the institutional-change strategy envisioned here. National policies and federal officials can—in fact, must—play a critical supporting role. It should not be a surprise to readers if I say at this juncture that I am hopeful, but worried. The chapters that follow deal with the policy and implementation lessons of the JOBS program.

10

Why Is Welfare So Hard to Reform?

In 1973, Henry Aaron wrote an influential book, *Why Is Welfare So Hard to Reform?* Not surprisingly for an economist, Aaron's focus was on incentives and analytical issues—specifically on the work-incentive and equity issues described earlier in the discussion of the Nixon Family Assistance Plan. I use the same title as Aaron's book for this chapter, which is about the *two fold* challenge of why it is so hard to reform welfare. Yes, the structure of the benefits matters, but so too does the management dimension.

In chapter 1, I contrasted the *income* and *employment* approaches to welfare reform. The basic choice is between giving hungry people fish and teaching them to fish. People taught to fish eventually can fend for themselves; people given fish always need more. The fact of the matter, however, is that politically in the United States this is not an either/or proposition. All major welfare reforms are two-dimensional. Politicians appear to feel this is essential. Moreover, the intellectual choice between the two positions (the income strategy and the employment strategy) is not as clear as is often portrayed. The aim of income strategies to reform welfare is to provide what economists call "a smooth benefits' curve" whereby a person on welfare loses a limited amount of money (say fifty cents out of a dollar in benefits) for every additional dollar earned. Such a 50 percent welfare-reduction rate is seen as an incentive for able-bodied welfare recipients of working age to get in and stay in the labor force.

On the other hand, proponents of the employment strategy for welfare reform argue that the key to helping welfare family heads is services. A person on welfare faces barriers to self-support that few people who have never experienced poverty and welfare can understand. Her basic skills (literacy and arithmetic) are likely to be limited, as are her job skills and her self-confidence. She needs help. So do her children. Child care while a welfare family head is in school is an essential need when considering employment strategies for AFDC family heads, most of whom are single women with children.

The history of welfare policy can be portrayed in terms of debates between these two ideas. The income approach emphasizes the behavior of individual recipients in response to the structure of welfare benefits. On the other hand, the employment approach emphasizes the behavior of the bureaucracy to provide job-related services. When examined up close and in practice, however, the distinction between the two approaches becomes muted. The new-style workfare approach embodied in the JOBS program, for example, has the character of both a service strategy and a back-door negative income tax.

There is already evidence that in some higher-benefit states the operation of new-style workfare increases the proportion of welfare family heads who have earnings, which is precisely what negative income tax plans are supposed to do. In Michigan, the proportion of AFDC recipients with earned income doubled during the period of my field visits. The rate was 8 percent statewide in 1984 and 16.1 percent in 1989. The numbers are even more impressive when the two large cities in Michigan (Detroit and Flint, both of which have high concentrations of welfare cases) are eliminated from the analysis. Not counting Detroit and Flint, the proportion of AFDC cases with earned income was 27.3 per cent in Michigan in 1988.[1]

These data are for the period of five years after the start-up of Michigan's MOST program. It is true that the MOST program, as portrayed by state officials, did not represent a major shift from past practice, and it is also true that the improved employment picture in Michigan undoubtedly had an effect on the rise in the number of working AFDC family heads. Still, in those cases where new-style workfare programs involve a stronger signal about the value of work and the availability of training and job opportunities, one would expect welfare recipients to move into the labor force in greater numbers. In many cases where this happens (especially in higher-benefit states) recipients continue to receive some welfare support, though at a reduced level.

In addition to its work emphasis and job-facilitation features, the JOBS program provides up to one year of "transitional" medical care and child care benefits for welfare family heads who go to work after a family is no longer entitled to an AFDC cash payment. Presumably the opportunity for the continuation of these two critical benefits reduces an AFDC family head's nervousness over entering the labor force. State officials in Michigan told me they believed the combination of a stronger work signal and training and other job-related services, plus the prospect of transitional benefits, contributed to the rise in the number of working AFDC family heads. These comments apply both to welfare heads who retain some (but lowered) AFDC benefits and those who eventually go off the rolls after they go to work but continue for one year to receive transitional Medicaid and child care benefits.

BACK TO BASICS

We need at this juncture to return to welfare basics. According to the law in some states and to the official explanation of the way AFDC works, a welfare family head initially faces a high—67 percent or more—marginal benefit-reduction rate. This reduction rate means she loses sixty-seven cents in welfare benefits for each additional dollar she earns. Critics point out that the extra transportation and work-related costs incurred by going to work add to this marginal benefit-reduction rate, as does the fact that her earnings are taxable. If you assign even modest estimates to these additions to the 67 percent reduction rate, it can be shown (or at least so it is claimed) that a welfare family head in some situations actually will be worse off if she goes to work. I have already noted that a welfare family head is likely to face reentry problems if and when she loses or leaves a job and needs to go back on welfare. Supporters of negative income tax schemes argue that all of this adds up to an indictment of the AFDC system, arguing that you cannot force people to act in ways that go against this inexorable arithmetic. But wait a minute.

The operations of welfare systems do not work the way experts often say they do. Many factors enter into the calculations that are not readily apparent from reading the law and regulations. A study by the Manpower Demonstration Research Corporation of case files for AFDC recipients in four states found that welfare-reduction rates varied widely and that they were likely to be lower than many observers expect. The MDRC study found that the average welfare-reduction rate was 44 percent in Baltimore, 49 percent in West Virginia, 56 percent in San Diego, and 65 percent in Virginia.[2] Only one of the four states (Virginia) was found to be significantly above the 50 percent welfare-reduction rate suggested as the goal of many of the welfare reformers who favor negative income tax or guaranteed income schemes. Other studies show similar findings.

We need to double back and add to this discussion the fact that new-style workfare programs put in place under the 1988 Family Support Act change the arithmetic of welfare by providing one year of transitional Medicaid and child care benefits in cases in which a welfare family head earns enough to go off the AFDC rolls. Other factors are also important in this connection. Food stamp benefits continue in many cases in which poor families are in the labor force, and other subsidies come into play, such as the earned income tax credit (EITC), which increases family income in this situation. The bottom line is that there are incentives for poor family heads to work. Add to this the observations I made earlier about the research findings that show that welfare family heads want to work.[3]

Returning to the Michigan case, experts in this state make still another point. The labor market has changed. The increase in the number of lower-paid service jobs (often part-time jobs with low and limited fringe benefits) has important consequences for welfare policy. It may over time cause the mission of the AFDC system to change so that it operates *both* as a safety net and as a work supplement. The combination of new-style workfare sending a stronger prowork signal and the transitional benefits provided in the Family Support Act, along with other available benefits such as EITC and food stamps plus the kinds of changes in the labor market I have just discussed, suggest that we may now be entering a new period for welfare policy. We may be evolving toward a system of family-income supports for low wages that, while lacking simplicity, serves the dual role of being *both* a minimum-income safety net *and* a work supplement. Increasingly, what we have is a *multiprogram* system that, it can be argued, is adaptable to changing family needs and circumstances. This is more true than is often recognized by critics who long for simplicity and neatness, neither of which really fits today's complex economic and social environment.

The biggest single step that could be taken to alleviate incentive problems for welfare families would be to reform health programs so that Medicaid benefits are not categorically linked to AFDC recipients. Most proposed national health care financing plans are universal. They cover everyone, so decisions about going on or staying on AFDC would not be affected by whether a family is receiving Medicaid benefits. In too many situations at present, a young woman becomes a welfare recipient in the hospital. Hospital admitting officers are quick to offer and arrange for payment by the state for new unmarried single mothers, making them recipients of Medicaid benefits before they are discharged and in the process making them the heads of new welfare families. Four or five years later, if and when the welfare family head sees a chance to go off welfare, a major deterrent is likely to be her worry that she will lose Medicaid benefits.

An added political factor needs to be taken into account here. Politically, I have always felt that the pluralist policy-making process in the United States is an important reason why we have a correspondingly *pluralist* welfare system. The various programs just mentioned have different constituencies—cash assistance, food stamps, health benefits, housing assistance, child care. This is not unique to the United States but it is distinctive of both our policies and our welfare system. The outcome may be more aid than otherwise would be the case for what is unfortunately a very unpopular group, even among the poor— broken or never formed (mostly black and Hispanic) welfare families headed by an able-bodied, working-age adult. If this group was aided under a single, high visibility, national program—such as a negative income tax—the temptation to cut benefits in conservative periods might very well be harder to resist than is the case with the decentralized multibenefit approach we now have.

This part of the analysis may be hard going for readers not familiar with the intricacies of welfare policy. But the points made are critical and could soon again be controversial. In chapter 3, I referred to the criticism of the Family Support Act by conservative welfare expert Charles Murray who believes that transitional benefits will add people to the welfare rolls. As a result, he expects liberal politicians eventually to make these benefits available to all working poor persons, whether or not they are just coming off AFDC. In the meantime, Murray also worries that people who are not on welfare and lose their jobs will decide to go on welfare in order to obtain one year of health and child care benefits. We do not know whether this will happen. Much depends on the way the 1988 act plays out over time. If in the long run JOBS services, transitional Medicaid, and child care benefits are provided to a larger number of working poor family heads, there will be more reason for poor family heads to go to work or continue working, which (while Charles Murray does not like it) is precisely what the income strategy for welfare reform is supposed to do.

In short, we could yet see changes in labor-market behavior due to the Family Support Act. When we look back ten years from now, we may attribute very important far-reaching—although as yet imperfectly perceived—changes in welfare programs to this new law. The potential is there, though in 1992, as this book is being written, it is hard to predict whether it will be fulfilled. Why?

I return to my theme. All this depends heavily on our old friend, implementation. Without knowing the way the implementation process will ultimately play out, we are hard put to say how far the new-style workfare systems of the 1990s will go. We should give the Family Support Act a chance to be the core of a new, changed welfare system for poor families. Other similar laws have been enacted in the past to do this, although none quite so far-reaching. My hope is that there will be greater seriousness over time about the implementation of the JOBS program. This is needed and yet is not easy to do. *It is an important reason why welfare is so hard to reform.*

CHAPTER

11

Changing the Way We Work in the Shadow Land

This book began with a quotation from a poem by T. S. Eliot, "The Hollow Men," about the distance between the idea and the reality, the motion and the act, in what Eliot called the shadow land. My iron-rod theme, to cite Henry James again, is that this shadow land of policy implementation is the neglected dimension of United States governance. Indeed, it is not surprising that the competitive United States political system produces an implementation vacuum. There are so many players engaged in making policy in the United States that there is not enough energy left over in the political process to follow up on what happens to policy after it is made. Implementation gets short shrift. As one decision is made, the next issue comes to the fore. Questions about what happened to a policy just made get pushed aside.

The JOBS program is an agent for institutional change. The aim is to change the signals and services—*the behavior*—of state and local welfare bureaucracies. We put up a new flag. Will the troops salute? Will they march? If they don't, then a lot of energy and effort have been wasted and we are kidding ourselves if we think anything will really change.

The way top elected officials recruit, select, deploy, and support the heads of large public agencies has an immense amount to do with what happens to programs such as JOBS. The critical task of making connections between setting policy goals and carrying them out depends on the appointed officials who head major government agencies in the domestic sector. Compared with other governmental systems, the United States system is remarkable for having a large number of appointed officials (secretaries, commissioners, and their various deputies and assistants). Although not everyone will agree, I believe the idea that these officials should push policy ideas into the implementation process is fully consistent with democratic theory. Unless the values that politicians stand for are reflected in the way government operates, all the new legislation in the world is for naught. When people vote for politicians they have every right to believe that what those politicians promise to do is what they will do. It is not beyond the wit of United States citizens to reform our governmental systems so that this objective can be more easily achieved. But it is not enough to make changes at the edges. More basic reforms in government operations are needed, reforms that modify our civic culture.

MODIFYING THE CIVIC CULTURE

The implementation problems of new-style workfare and similar domestic programs—whether they be social, physical, educational, or environmental—are rooted in the reward system of United States politics and the structure and character of our state and local government. Politicians have reached a new low standing. Campaigns dominated by big money, telegenic candidacies, sound bites, and spin doctors have fueled a reaction. The public's willingness to throw incumbents out, limit terms, and cut government spending reflects a widespread feeling that elected officials are toying with our emotions, talking down to us, and not really caring about the way government operates. Bureaucratic rigidity and the acceptance by workers in many governments of the attitude that nothing can change, that every interest group should fight to keep what it has and prevent anyone else's gain, have fostered a spirit of resignation and time-serving. Robert Behn's book about the Massachusetts ET program is called *Leadership Counts*. This is my main point too—the need for leaders who can serve as change agents, stick with the job, focus on management, and help create a positive tone toward governmental accomplishment. In much the same way, David Osborne and Ted Gaebler make the case for a change in the style and spirit of government operations.

> What we are describing is nothing less than a shift in the basic model of governance used in America. This shift is under way all around us, but because we are not looking for it—because we assume that all governments have to be big, centralized, and bureaucratic—we seldom see it. We are blind to the new realities, because they do not fit our preconceptions.
>
> What we need most if this revolution is to succeed, in other words, is a new framework for understanding government, a new way of thinking about government—in short, a new *paradigm*. [1]

The thesis of their book, entitled *Reinventing Government,* is that we need a new entrepreneurial spirit in government, which Osborne and Gaebler believe can transform the public sector. Osborne and Gaebler's book contains an important subtheme, an idea that is central, and appropriately so, in the private sector. I refer to the idea that business organizations should be customer-oriented: Who are we trying to serve? What is their view? What are their wants and needs?

Of course, customer satisfaction is not the same in the private and public sectors. Consumers can decide whether or not to buy a Madonna disc. But many of the products and services of government are for everyone, including people who don't want them or don't want the same services or products that someone else wants. There are many different groups of customers. They can't all be satisfied.

This constant bargaining process over what economists call "public goods" is bound to be intense. The more controversial and emotional the issue, the more intense the debate. There are clear limits to the analogy between the public and private sectors that in my opinion place a high premium on politically skillful, mission-oriented leadership in the critical arena of public policy implementation.

The point I have just made about caring more about implementation is key for both of the two main types of reforms discussed in this chapter—*leadership* changes and *institutional* changes. It is rare for a governor or mayor (and even rarer in the case of a president of the United States) to give management top attention; political leaders give little time and effort to implementation. Yet, I believe it is not too much to hope for to bring about changes that give greater emphasis to performance and results in governmental operations. There are features of the United States political system, brought to life by the case studies in this book, that suggest strategies that can cause this to happen.

One such feature, as I have already noted, involves the type of people who run large public bureaucracies in the United States. Most of them are appointed officials accountable to the politicians who selected them. In comparison with other countries, government in the United States stands out for its large number of appointed officials who serve in this way. The federal establishment has 3,000 appointive positions exempted from the civil service. States and large cities also have several layers of appointed officials. United States government has been faulted in this respect by critics who think we should rely more on civil servants. This theory, which stresses "neutral competence" by civil servants, reached its zenith in the United States in the late nineteenth century. Civil services were created at the national level and by many states in response to excesses of the spoils system—government jobs being used on a wholesale basis for political payoffs. Nevertheless the political-executive model has prevailed and in my view is the correct model for the United States.

The role of appointed officials in state government is especially critical for domestic affairs. State governments have major responsibilities for structuring and managing a wide range of domestic programs in a way that makes it logical for them to have the lead role in policy implementation. The services that need to be expanded and connected for new-style workfare, for example, are not the kinds of governmental activities that can be micromanaged from Washington. Although the national government provides financial support for these and other social services, predominant responsibility for structuring and managing these kinds of social services is lodged with states, which administer these services directly or supervise their administration by local governments.

MANAGING PROGRAMS SUCH AS NEW-STYLE WORKFARE

The way policies such as new-style workfare are transmitted to the bureaucracy involves sensitive questions of values. Many workers in local welfare offices and associated nonprofit organizations that provide social services have different views on welfare issues from those of central policymakers and the public. In the New Jersey and Detroit examples discussed earlier, local workers were found to have a decidedly negative attitude toward sanctions and community work experience. The idea that government should force poor people to do something—even if it is in exchange for cash benefits or services of value to them—raises a red flag for many social workers and advocates of the poor.

These concerns, however, are not reflected in public opinion or at higher levels of government. Policy makers in the welfare field at the national and state levels focus their attention on the opinions of people outside the welfare system. This creates a problem of *credibility*. If welfare programs coddle the poor rather than motivate them, taxpayers will continue to be unhappy and will take politicians' promises about getting people off welfare (a constant refrain) with a grain of salt.

The issue for public management is the obvious one. Unless welfare workers' attitudes toward the aims and elements of new-style workfare and other similarly politically sensitive policy changes can be changed, politicians will adopt policies that cannot be implemented or at least cannot be implemented without inordinate effort. The more controversial a policy is, the more likely it is that the use of political skill by agency heads to influence and change worker attitudes will be essential to its implementation. There are many areas of social policy in which delicate and complicated political bargains are made. The need in these areas as I see it is for "*dual implementation strategies*." This phrase refers to the need on the one hand for political leadership in the implementation process and on the other for taking managerial considerations into account in policy formulation.

In Massachusetts, strong leadership on the part of political leaders had a major impact in changing the signals, substance, and services of the welfare bureaucracy. Contrary to my expectation, I found that the exhortation to "get people off of welfare" and the aggressive use of performance goals focused on this objective brought greater pressure to bear on the bureaucracy under the ET program in Massachusetts than was the case under the seemingly more obligatory work-welfare programs of other states. The commissioner of the Massachusetts Department of Public Welfare, Charles M. Atkins, and his staff played a strong role in the design and execution of the ET program. Atkins was assigned the lead in developing the ET program in the beginning of Michael Dukakis's second term as governor. He had had previous experience in the welfare field in Dukakis's first term and was in a good position after the four-year hiatus during which Dukakis was out of power to anticipate the challenge involved in implementing ET. In New Jersey, Commissioner of Human Services Drew Altman also had a major hand in enacting the legislation that established the REACH program. He and Associate Commissioner Dennis Beatrice stressed flexibility in dealing with the counties and brought senior career officials into the policy design process.

The same kinds of considerations apply to the flip side of this proposition: state political officials responsible for crafting policies such as new-style workfare should consult with experts in the career services about the difficulties likely to be encountered in implementation of their policies. If their plans for new services are overly ambitious or too rigid, and therefore the promises for success made to gain public support are too expansive, problems of shortfall and public frustration are bound to occur. Attention in advance to the experience of agency experts can help shape new policies to head off adjustments that otherwise have to be made (often with difficulty) later on. This is not to suggest that implementation can be trouble free, only that involving management experts in the policy-planning process can reduce the amount of "fixing" that needs to be done at a later time.

The way the state-local structure variable played out in New Jersey is an illustration of this point. The fact that the state policymakers who conceived the REACH program had to deal with a deep-seated home rule tradition and the confrontational politics of county welfare systems made the job of implementing new-style workfare much harder in New Jersey than in Massachusetts. A similar point can be made for California, which has the strongest new-style workfare program on paper among the five states I studied in the field. The GAIN program is explicit about the sequence of services, the sanctioning process, and the obligations of welfare family heads. Regrettably, the intense political jockeying that produced this elaborate policy compromise exacerbated problems of implementation.

THE CRITICAL ROLE OF AGENCY HEADS

As a society, we need to increase the quality of state and local managerial leadership. Appointed agency heads and their principal associates are the key to doing so. They can be professional politicians, but most are professionals in their field who come from other places, other agencies, businesses, or nonprofit organizations, or who move up through the ranks into appointed positions. The governmental system

as a whole needs to pay more attention to the role, salary, qualifica-
tions, performance, and tenure of these officials. These jobs offer excitement and a sense of fulfillment and service. The people who head
large state and local public agencies direct armies of professionals,
specialists, and line workers. They have an opportunity to make a mark
in ways that are critical to the well-being of their community.

But the downside for people considering these management challenges is formidable. Salaries and benefits for top managers have improved in some states but they still fall short of what good managers
can earn in the private sector. Moreover, the politics that swirl around
public agencies often make these jobs frustrating, hasten managerial
burn-out, and can even make these positions professionally risky. I
have in mind the damage that can be done to a manager's reputation
as a result of attacks from politicians and journalists who seek scape-
goats for the inability of government to deal with deepening social
problems such as family poverty and dysfunction, child abuse, crime,
drugs, and homelessness. Strict conflict-of-interest and financial-disclo-
sure laws add to the barriers that discourage people outside the public
sector from accepting appointive positions in government and taking
on these and other hard but critical challenges.

Career patterns vary in public management for different levels of
government. In the federal government, "inners and outers," who are
often amateurs in government, typically stay for two or three years and
then leave for what are often lucrative jobs outside government. The
prevalence of these in-and-out patterns caused Hugh Heclo to give the
title *Government of Strangers* to a book about high-level public service
in the federal government.[2] At the state and local levels, however, this
is not so much the case. Deborah Roberts of the University of Virginia
notes a pattern of what she calls "inners and arounders" in top state
management jobs. She writes not about a government of strangers, but
about "a government of acquaintances," referring to the people who
hold appointive jobs and then, after they finish a given assignment,
move to a different branch or agency or to a related position.[3] They
are in a sense professional political appointees.[4]

Although many top state appointees come from within the state and
are known to people in their field, there are instances in which governors and local officials recruit outside candidates for these positions. A
good case can be made for increasing external searches for fresh talent
for leadership posts, despite the fact that external searches are hard to
conduct. Most appointing officials (governors, big-city mayors, and

their staffs) do not have the skills, time, and contacts to mount national searches. The costs involved in using private search firms to perform this service are likely to be too high, or at least to be perceived as too high. One solution that I believe could make a difference would be for foundations to underwrite outside searches in key areas, either by setting up new organizations to provide this service or by paying the costs of obtaining this service from existing executive recruitment firms.[5]

Executive recruiters match the requirements of an employer with the skills and experience of potential candidates; there is an educational aspect to this process as well as a talent-scouting dimension. One of the main steps undertaken by executive recruiters in matching clients and prospects is to set up meetings for prospective appointees where they get a picture of the lay of the land and learn about key "stakeholders" (key legislators, other officials, heads of interest groups, etc.). In this process, potential new appointees also learn about the aims and style of the appointing official, be it a governor, mayor, cabinet secretary, or board or council. In this way skilled recruiters provide potential new appointees in advance with valuable insights about the background, interests, and aims of the major players and groups with whom they would interact. The recruiters can also do some proselytizing to help make sure that the men and women selected for appointive posts are committed to stay the course by serving for a substantial period.

However it is carried out, the appointment of top officials is one of the most critical tasks of elected officials at the outset of a new administration. Decisions have to be made about the values that should be stressed, how the people selected should relate to the appointing official and to each other, and how they should use their time. This last point is especially important. Unfortunately, elected officials tend to be preoccupied with tasks other than management. Dealing with the press, interest groups, and the legislature often takes precedence over managerial tasks.

This is not to say that devoting more time to implementation is enough. The implementation process, as we have seen, is often bound up by institutional barriers that make it hard to change the way governments function no matter how much time and energy are devoted to the task. The civil service in many jurisdictions has been overbuilt and has become ossified. If a governor or mayor appoints a new agency head who shares his or her ideas about a particular policy area, the opportunity for that official to pick and deploy subordinates with shared values and the right skills can be frustrated by civil service requirements. For example, in some states a "rule of three" requires career appointments to be made from a list of three people named by a panel that the appointing official does not control. A desire to move out or reassign a career official who does not share a new leader's ideas and goals can be prevented by other civil service rules that make it almost impossible to move or remove a senior career official. Sometimes eliminating positions or reorganizing a function can trigger a series of interlocking bumping steps that cause hundreds of people down the line to displace the person below them in a game of musical chairs that makes everyone miserable and insecure.

To add to these potential problems, the laws and rules for labor-management relations in government make unions a much more important factor in the public sector than in the private, adding another level of administrative complexity and rigidity. Likewise, rules to achieve across-the-board goals, such as environmental protection, workplace safety, and civil rights, can stymie managerial leadership. This is not because the rules themselves are a bad idea. Government in the United States is rule-bound for a reason; red tape for some is a cherished objective for others.

In recent years budget cuts have added institutional barriers in dealing with budget officials in the executive branch and in the legislature. The courts, too, are significant players in management in the social policy arena and in recent years have increasingly involved themselves in administration. Opponents of a given policy can go to court to prevent changes that agency managers seek. In fields such as corrections, mental hospitals, schools, and welfare, the influence of the courts often predominates over that of the other two branches of government.

Daniel Patrick Moynihan, a key figure in this book, once lamented that experts are "complexifiers" and sometimes only make the situation worse. True enough. Still, it would detract from my argument about giving more attention to implementation to imply that doing so is simple. This is not to say that the public sector is uniquely barrier-ridden, only that it is more barrier-ridden than the private sector. Corporate managers face many of the same types of obstacles, but often not as many and not to the degree found in government. Nor is this to say that elected chief executives in government do not care about what happens inside government. My experience indicates that there are many dedicated and caring elected politicians. I want to influence these officials to take advantage of untapped opportunities to affect and improve the performance of government by being shrewdly involved in implementation processes. I do not accept the argument that policy and administration are separate domains, that politicians should make policy and let civil servants carry it out. This distinction between policy and administration is patently false. *Policy takes shape in its execution*. If politicians stay out of this shadow land, they might as well stay home. If the idea of democracy means anything, it means that we elect people to advance our values. If politicians stop at the legislative water line, they run the risk of being of little relevance to what happens to ideas inside the world of government.

In the work I have done on this book I have given thought to institutional changes that could help elected and appointed officials penetrate and change administrative processes. Believing as I do in education, readers will not be surprised that one of my main ideas about how change can be facilitated involves schools—*public service academies for state and local appointed officials*.

PUBLIC SERVICE ACADEMIES

The United States government spends about one-quarter of a billion dollars a year on military academies and special schools for military officers all around the country. This includes the army, navy, and air force war colleges that train high-level officers. Why not peace colleges? I do not want to call them this, but the point is serious. We should set up institutions to identify and teach people who are or could be change agents in government about the special nature of the world of domestic public service. I would like to see the national government create a National Institute of Public Service that would operate regional educational institutions throughout the country to provide programs for people appointed to (or who could be appointed to) top management posts in state and local government. Each institution would have its own board. They could have different programs, although none of them should be degree-granting institutions. Programs should be of varying length, a month or two or three months being the usual length of stay. Public service academies could be associated with universities and draw on universities for instructional personnel, but I do not think they should be part of a university. They should be freestanding and restricted to their own student body. The instructional program should have courses on such subjects as

- the history and politics of the American governmental process,
- organization and personnel management,

- finances and budgeting,
- research and statistical analysis,
- law and ethics.

If such institutions are to be effective in increasing the supply of talented men and women to be agency managers in state and local government the most critical decisions about the operation of these public service academies would involve the admission of students. These students could be mid-careerists from business and other fields who seek new avenues of service. They could be managers in government ready to move up to more responsible posts, perhaps moving out of the career service to an appointive position. They could be individuals on whom governors or mayors or other political officials (both elected executives and appointed) set their sights for new challenges. They could be people just appointed to new posts who enter such a program for a month or two before they take on their new responsibilities. The admissions process should be flexible, that is, trying out different types of students over time. This requires savvy on the part of the leaders and boards of the public service academies. The long-term aim should be to create a democratic cadre of strong, able people who can move "in and around" in positions of managerial leadership in state and local government.

12

Ten Lessons

The experience recounted in this book about the implementation of domestic public policies suggests the following lessons.

1. *Implementation should get more attention.*

Politics must not stop at the legislative water's edge. Laws are agents for institutional change. In a change-resistant democratic political system such as ours, the intended tasks will not be accomplished unless leaders influence administrative processes. Few people have made the point as well and as strongly as children's activist Marion Wright Edelman, founder and president of the Children's Defense Fund. In an address at the John F. Kennedy School of Government at Harvard University in 1987, Edelman urged the new graduates to "pay attention to the nitty-gritty steps of implementation." Said Edelman, "Passing a law or drafting a regulation or issuing an RFP, is the easiest part of a change process. Making it work. Informing the public. And assisting and monitoring local enforcement, protecting budgets in a sustained manner, and getting and training sensitive and skilled personnel to administer it in a compassionate way are all important parts of the change process."[1]

2. *Strike while the iron is hot.*

Appointed policy officials should take advantage of their honeymoon period to create momentum by doing things early that often are much harder to do once the excitement of a new beginning has passed. When new public managers look around at the players and organizations in their policy network, they often find competitors for the benefits they can provide. Resistance is down, constraints are lowered. Uncertainty about who will gain under the new order provides a moment for winning support for managerial and organizational changes that in many instances will be harder, if not impossible, to achieve at a later time. This is not to say that one can throw caution to the wind in early action. Each step along the way involves calculations about later possible costs. My point is only that the managerial cost-benefit equation is likely to be better early on.

3. *Institutions matter.*

In a different context, Jean Monnet, the pioneer of European union, said "Nothing is possible without men; nothing is lasting without institutions."[2] The point is that agency managers who operate as change agents have to think strategically about what they will leave behind—the organizational, personnel, and intergovernmental structures that can sustain the effects of their actions. This challenge to leave a legacy often requires a team approach by an elected chief executive and his or her major appointees. In addition, it mitigates against selecting too large a number of purposes. The example of new-style workfare suggests that if an agency head seeks, as in this case, to change the signals and services of the welfare bureaucracy, the attempt to do so should not be swamped by having too many other competing high-level purposes. Drew Altman's approach in New Jersey, where he selected five main policy- and institutional-change goals at the outset of his tenure and emphasized them frequently, is a good way to avoid overcommitment and maintain the focus on institutional-change objectives.

4. *People matter too.*

Good management is dependent on the selection and deployment of good people. A public official (elected or appointed) can only deal on a regular basis with a relatively small number of people—seven and maybe ten close and trusted (or at least pretty much trusted) associates. They have to be people one can talk to, with whom a leader can communicate quickly and clearly and in a way that is comfortable (even fun some of the time). Picking and deploying this core management group and forging relationships that make it work are vital to the art

of policy implementation. Political scientist Richard Elmore says organizations should be seen as instruments for fulfilling goals: "Organizations can be remarkably effective devices for working out difficult
public problems, but their use requires an understanding of the reciprocal nature of authority relations. . . . Very little can be done about
the problem [the complexity of joint action] if analysts and policy
makers persist in viewing implementation as a hierarchically ordered
set of authority relationships." [3]

5. *Stick around.*

This lesson for policy implementation is easier to state than to carry
out. Public managers who care about putting a new policy or program
in place need five years or more in a particular role or agency if they
want their efforts to bear fruit, not just for one season, but for many.

6. *Set goals that can be used as the basis for rewards and punishments.*

Reward and punish. But especially do the former. Reward good
performance. The rewards of public service in America are few and far
between. Leaders in high-visibility managerial positions in the public
sector can make an important contribution simply by shining a spotlight on key objectives and good performance. In Massachusetts, the
governor and his staff papered people's walls with awards. One can be
cynical about this, but in fact it worked.

7. *Avoid being mired in details.*

Good management leadership in the complex world of government
is not micromanagement. It requires trust in others. It requires the
ability to delegate and in the process to influence and motivate people
inside large organizations.

8. *Respect careerists but watch them.*

Civil service systems can be stultifying. Dealing with this key management variable is as challenging as any I know for people who want
to exercise leadership in government. An appointed official cannot get
very far without the trust and help of key people in the permanent
bureaucracy. Smart agency heads send positive signals about the importance of the career service, but this does not mean they should just
"go with the flow" of civil service procedures and requirements. They
should use their best efforts and most finely honed political skills to
move people with shared values and with whom they have good
chemistry into jobs for purposes they most care about. This calls for a
high order of skill in the selection and deployment of career personnel.

9. *Be shrewd about relations with the legislature.*

In the United States, legislative bodies are very powerful. The first
article of the U.S. Constitution establishes the Congress and sets forth

the enumerated powers of the national government. Congress refers to itself as "the First Branch" and acts accordingly. States have similar constitutions and their legislatures often behave in a like manner. Although it is important for public managers to be loyal to the official who appointed them, often this cannot be accomplished unless they also cultivate good relationships with the legislature.

10. *Do what has to be done.*

The literature about public administration tends to make light of conflict. The main need, we are told, is for greater understanding and coordination. Political leaders are often chastised for being heavy-handed and impatient, pushing ahead with their plans without allowing enough time for consultation. Yes, there are situations in which the challenge for a policy manager is to persuade in order to bring career bureaucrats on board for the implementation of major policy changes. But time is precious. Leaders who want to make changes cannot wait forever. Sometimes the right thing to do is to take decisive action even if it involves strong measures to discipline an uncooperative career official, organization, or associate. I realize full well that there are limits to such actions. They can backfire and create an atmosphere in which leadership is not possible. In response to an earlier book I wrote that dealt with many of the themes in this one, but was focused on the national government, a political scientist wrote a whole book of refutation.[4] As far as I could tell, his main problem with my position was that it is not nice enough. He called for greater understanding, more respect for people, and the like. This is all well and good. But it is not the only way to govern. This is a problem with some of my academic colleagues who are desk- and book-bound. Firm action is sometimes the right tactic for policy managers who want to make a difference. Politics, said Mr. Dooley, "ain't beanbag!"

13

Advice to a New Commissioner

This final chapter is in the form of letters to a hypothetical friend just named as an agency head in the government of a large state. The letters are personal, for her eyes only. The governor (I call him Franklin Smith) who appointed her was recently elected for the first time to a four-year term. He lacks political experience, has lots of ideas, lots of leftover campaign advisers, and an uncertain mandate. Ann, a former colleague, was recommended to Governor Smith by one of his college classmates. Most recently, she had been vice president for research of the state university.

Dear Ann [commissioner-designate],

First of all, good for you on being named to Franklin Smith's cabinet. I can't think of a more worthy outlet for your talent, energy, and commitment. I wish I could have gotten together with you when you were here last month, but I couldn't squirm out of my commitment to that London conference. I write this letter for your eyes only. It is informal and personal, even whimsical in places. Take if for what it is, the ruminations of a friend. Pardon me for making it so long, but I was swamped this week. Anyway, you can read this selectively.

You asked if I had ever met Frank Smith. I met him once. He seemed pleasant, earnest, but uninformed about the state and major players, especially in the legislature. His public service record is good, but not long. His business experience is impressive but can lead him astray I fear. Charles Gray once told me he thinks Frank Smith has the attention span of a three-year-old, but I attribute that to Chuck's bad experience with Frank on the Joint Commission on Management.

Of course, our new governor's video sense is uncanny; he is a wonderful spokesman. This is an asset, but may be a liability too—at least for you. From what I can tell, Smith has little interest in public policy, the budget, or agency operations.

This brings up a larger question we have discussed before. It worries me that television politics has soured our governmental process. Telegenic candidates with celebrity status, aided by spin doctors who produce sound bites, have made government unpopular because of the way it plays on people's emotions. Candidates talk down to the public. No wonder citizens are frustrated and angry.

Frank Smith's campaign was better than most. He seemed to be trying to get at central issues. But the advertising patina was dominant, and in the final analysis this gubernatorial race, like the last one, fueled a turn-off by the public.

What irritates me about this is that the most notorious celebrity politicians set the tone for government. Their superficial treatment of issues does more than hurt their image. It demeans people in government who are caring and hardworking—people like you for instance. The infection is deep. The unsung heroes who do the Lord's work at the local level in government and in nonprofit groups running housing projects, drug treatment, special schools are tarnished with the same broad brush. I particularly find offensive the bureaucracy bashing of Bush and Reagan who played on the public's discontent over the cost of government. We need to find ways, as you and I have discussed before, to shine a spotlight on the real and good work of government. The public looks at government through a telescope. If only we could get people to use a microscope instead and look at the fine, committed people in and around government who work hard because they care about what they are doing. I know you will work on this.

I warned you at the outset this would be a discursive letter. You can read this part quickly. You know my feelings. In the final analysis, I worry that Frank Smith will use his office in a way that reinforces, rather than combats, these increasingly strong and bad television tendencies.

There oughta be a law: How about a law prohibiting any politician or group of politicians from purchasing less than five minutes of television or radio air time? Can I count on your support?

You asked me to recommend books on management. I like the Peters and Waterman book, *In Search of Excellence*. Even though it is about the private sector, Peters and Waterman have terrific insights about how people behave and can be motivated. They are skeptical of fancy analysis, the rational-actor model, and elaborate planning. Their needling about business schools is right on, for example where they talk about "paralysis by analysis." As we have discussed many times, management at the top in both business and government is an art form. It is a function of style and situation.

You mentioned the book by David Osborne and Ted Gaebler on "reinventing government." This book's contribution is to give us *hope* that government can change, be more flexible and creative. This is what they call being "*entrepreneurial*." The book is upbeat and readable. The examples they use are encouraging. Osborne and Gaebler build up the idea that government can change. But it isn't easy. Underneath and critical to these good intentions are myriads of rigid institutional conditions that will make your life as a commissioner hard some days and that you and your colleagues in the administration must try to change if real leadership is going to be possible and sustained.

You know my refrain: *Care about implementation*. Push policies into the bureaucracy. Pick the values and policies you care about, and that the governor likes and stands for. Stay the course. Don't come back until you have really made an impact and you feel it will be sustained. It will take the full four years—maybe five. I am sure you expected me to say this. At least, this part of my letter is concise.

I remember what you said after you had that stint at the health department, "The Devil IS in the details." You were discouraged by the failure of Dan Crumpet's bill, not about getting it enacted but having it make a difference inside the government after all the hoopla.

You have to take advantage of "Big Mo." Strike while the iron is hot now—early in the administration. Do the tough things now. Don't be afraid to tell Shirley she is not in your plans and that you will help her find something else. If she doesn't move, you should remove her. People know she has been slowing everything down and undermining morale. You will get credit for this.

But the other two people you mentioned are more of a problem. They have ties to William Bennett in the House. Nonetheless, I am inclined to think they should be moved down or out—and quickly. You know the old joke about my giving you three envelopes when you start a new job. Number one, announce a bold new program. Number two, reorganize. Number three, make three envelopes. For Seth Adams and Emma, I'd reorganize them down, or better yet out. It's time. The agency is top-heavy and deputy-heavy. Reorganization, as Herbert Kaufman used to say, is a political thing. There is no right way to organize anything. One of its best applications is for people-moving. You can do this. You don't need a law. Don't ask the governor. And, whatever you do, don't ask the Budget Bureau.

I am told our former student (you had him in class) Terry Winston is good and that he will be Frank's chief policy person. There are a few people like Terry you should level with. Not fully of course. I mean tell him a lot and talk with him about lots of things candidly. But keep in the back of your mind that there are some ideas, purposes, dislikes you have that you should keep completely to yourself. You are good at this. It is a critical skill in government. As Henry Adams said in his autobiography, "a friend in power is a friend lost." It's too bad, yet pretty much true. Be careful. The capitol is a rough place, especially after the euphoria of a new regime wears off. You know what is coming down the road—tight budgets and slow growth. So what else is new?

Some days it is best to lie low and say as little as possible, because if you act or react you may mess up. Pacing yourself and keeping your spirits up is a challenge in itself.

Going back to my point about the Osborne-Gaebler book, there are rigidities that make it hard to be "entrepreneurial"—to move and sustain movement in government. The civil service is terribly overbuilt and rigid. I worry a lot about this. Government unions, which compete with the civil service, are stronger than in the private sector. You need to know a lot about these two systems. Knowledge in these areas—like deep, detailed knowledge about your budget—is something you cannot delegate.

As for your own staff, make it small and rely a lot on the deputies. Try to work well with your team. Pick some new deputies. Signal that you are in charge. Make good choices. You can do this, though not easily. However, few things are more important.

Be careful not to make your core staff and deputies group too homogeneous—not all "PR" types, or economic-analysis types, or political types, or close legal reasoners. Try to get a little of each of these different perspectives so that each time you have a crisis or a major opportunity you get advice that reflects the different dimensions of the question—managerial, analytical, legal, political, press, hardball, etc. Yes, you do need someone who is not afraid to be tough. But not too many people inclined this way or, for that matter, any other way.

Your instincts, judgment, commitment are strong qualities. You can have a lot of confidence going in. You have a wonderful chance if you stick around long enough to make and leave your mark—as we used to say, "to be a change agent."

Flexibility and surprises. You know I believe good managers are adaptive, iterative, situational. Also, get out and about. Show your face to the troops. Visit a lot of sites early on. When you do, meet the neighbors—the local politicos, people from other agencies, the local press.

And remember what we both said on the Joint Task Force. When you are new, you can ask dumb questions. Get a lot of information early. After about six months, dumb questions look like precisely that—*dumb* questions. Don't let people talk your ear off. Don't go to meetings that aren't going to accomplish anything. Get a person you like and trust to run your schedule. Keep working on TV. It's the world now. You do well. You can do even better: "Short, sweet, don't repeat." Just like a conversation with someone. You might get coaching on this. For goodness sakes, don't let your press aide have her head all the time. Susan Childress is good. I remember her from the Eton campaign, but sometimes she amazes me by her bad instincts.

As for the Bates law, you and I worked hard to get it passed. But that is only the beginning. Remember when Don Prime taught Government 101? He used Wally Sayre's model.* Wally used the metaphor of the "wheel of government" to show how fluid, open, and fragmented the American political system is. He gave a wonderful talk on the wheel of government. Too bad he never wrote it up. Wally said you could put anyone in the center of the wheel—a bureau chief, secretary, assistant secretary, etc. Then he showed the spokes—the Congress, the courts, the White House, the press, interest groups, parties, and so on. Each time a question comes up, Sayre said, the person in the center of the wheel has options of who to call, ask to help, work with, etc. The bureau chief comes in first thing in the morning and finds a stack of pink phone slips. Who does she call? You could study influence, Wally said, just by checking to see who was called first, second, third, or never. Note his "ABC's" in bottom left of the chart. They are wonderful. Nobody in the world has a political system like ours!

Anyway, I digress about all this because I promised a long letter and now I'm having fun. You are in the center of the wheel. But so are others. You can do a lot, but the gears can get frozen too.

I am ambivalent about how many goals you should have and how explicit you should be about them. In some situations, it makes sense to have a few goals and really press them. Other times, it serves you better to have a lot of goals so you can be sure to have some successes. At still other times, it is better to keep to yourself what you care about. This is more a matter of personal style and the situation than anything else. But generally I would say that as a new commissioner I think you should—as the state lottery says— "pick five." Focus your goals on *substance*. I think this is desirable in order to stand for something and to husband your resources and use them for what you really care about and want to leave behind. If you let people around you know what you want, they can help you. And if they don't like what you want or don't like you, at least you find out where they stand, and that is a useful input.

Your comments, letters, and speeches matter. Structures and regulations matter too. The sad truth of all of our public management studies, both yours and mine, is that there is no one secret answer

---

* Sayre is a real person; he was a professor of political science at Columbia University. The chart shown here was prepared by Walter Held, formerly on the staff of the Brookings Institution, on the basis of a talk often given by Wallace Sayre.

FIGURE 13.1

The Wallace S. Sayre Model of the Federal Decision-making System [a]

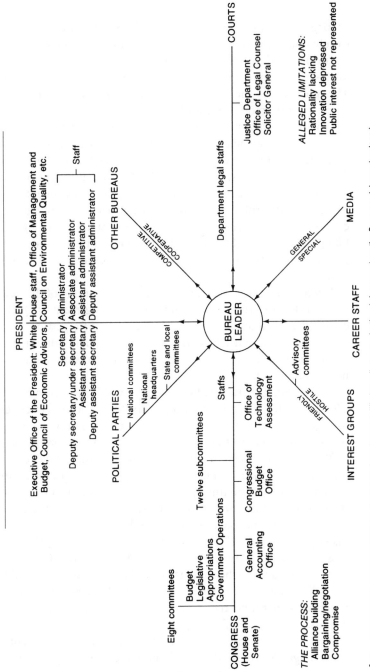

[a] The presidential and congressional lines of influence have been modified to reflect organizational changes since the Sayre model was developed.

or magic bullet other than the need to know about, care about, and closely follow the ideas and programs you want to stand for. You can't do everything. You have to be *selective*. What is it we used to say about how much time and effort it takes to turn an ocean liner? The other side of that is that once you turn it, the next guy has just as much work to do to turn it back.

One other subject: As commissioner, you have a full plate. But there is also an agenda for the administration as a whole. What will Frank leave behind? I urge you and Ross Greenberg at Budget and Terry Winston to push for *"systemic"* reforms. I already mentioned the civil service. You should work on this; the appointment process and civil service rules are ridiculous. Raw talent is discouraged, even abused, in government—at least in our state. That's a good bumper sticker: "Fight Talent Abuse in Government!" Getting at this requires subtle, persistent, clever strategies to reform institutions.

While I am at it, I would like to take a shot at one of the new panaceas for government—Total Quality Management (TQM). Because it has been useful in business as a method for getting people involved and committed to their work, many public administration experts now see it as a new "magic bullet" for government too. I urge caution on this.

The essential character of government is different from business. There are many more actors and players. Our Madisonian governmental system was built to provide wide access. This was seen as a way to avoid abuses of power, which it does in many good ways.

What we most need in government is leadership, direction, a mission that workers can identify with and feel like they are part of. I am all in favor of getting agency staff on board, but I don't think the way to do it in government is by setting up elaborate new TQM hoops for people to jump through. We already have too many process-type red tape systems in government. TQM in business adds a set of hoops. Adopting a carbon copy of TQM in government is wrongheaded. This would only exacerbate problems of gridlock and the frustration of many government workers that things don't get done the way they are supposed to, the way it is promised that they will be *implemented*.

You need to be creative about relations with the permanent staff of your agency. We need to work on "continuous-improvement" systems, not just one-shot dramatic reforms. There are many terrific people who can help you get on this track. You need to stroke some folks, and challenge others. And some people need to be threatened—sometimes not too gently, especially recalcitrants who see every new commissioner as a part-timer they don't have to take seriously. But whatever you do, don't buy TQM hook, line, and sinker. It was not made in heaven for government.

The same advice about learning and thinking creatively about basic systems applies to the budget process. It is overbearing and top-heavy. You and your fellow agency heads should convince Frank Smith to give you room, that you will help him and help each other if he does. Budgeting is the spinal column of good government, the best central decision system. You have to avoid having too many decision systems and having staff functions kill off substance and serious work. If our new governor is smart about this, he will use the budget process as his core decision system and rely heavily on you and your fellow commissioners to make it work for him. He mustn't fall victim to the common tendency to try to have budget examiners and his own staff run everything. He will get killed by the details if he does.

Labor-management relations is another systems problem area. No one stands up to the unions in government. This is unfair to them. It isn't their fault we cave in all the time.

A friend of mine has a terrific way to make a point that is critical in jobs like yours. He talks about the distinction between leadership and management. Management, he says, is doing things right. Leadership, on the other hand, is *doing the right things*. This is your moment for leadership!

Hang in there. Laugh a little. Remember, your friends and old colleagues are proud of you. We forgive you in advance for anything we don't like or that goes wrong. Public service is a high calling, but not an easy one.

Yours truly,

Dick

P.S. You'll never guess what just happened. Just as I was finishing this letter to you, I got a call from Frank Smith, of all people. He is going to be on campus Wednesday. He is meeting with the chancellor, and suggested the two of us have lunch after that. I will let you know how it goes. I'll write you another confidential letter.

Dear Ann,

He showed up. No entourage. Just Frank Smith. We had a long lunch at the faculty club. We sat in the corner, and no one bothered us.

You could have fooled me. Remember I said I didn't think Frank had much interest in being governor—just getting to be governor—and that Chuck Gray said his attention span is very limited. Well, I think I should revise my opinion.

Frank asked me right off the bat, "How do you move the ocean liner, how do you get the government to change the way it operates?" (Those were his actual words.) I told him most of what you would expect. I said you have to pick good and strong commissioners who share your ideas and values and give them room to operate and also give them a fair amount of your time. I told him I thought he had already made some good choices, and mentioned you, Ray, Richard, and Arthur, among others. I told him what I knew about each person—strengths, weaknesses, attention span, ability to project, political smarts, management sophistication. Of course, I gave you high marks.

Then we talked about the agencies, the politics, the legislative egos involved, and the way a governor should choose the areas he most cares about. Frank surprised me. He knows a good deal more than I thought about the lay of the land and the land mines. The two subjects we talked about next were his personal staff and the use of staff offices (budget, civil service, general services, etc.) vis-à-vis the line agencies.

I was very direct. I said, If you try to micromanage from the governor's office, you will get killed. The little stuff will come to the top, the big issues will sink to oblivion. You have to trust and know your commissioners. Good eh? But I really believe it. You have to care about what happens to policies after they are made. You have to encourage and help commissioners to be "entrepreneurial," creative, affirmative, engaged with the bureaucracy if you're going to change its tone and motivate its most talented, committed people.

I said Terry Winston can be a great source of support but only as a connector and facilitator. If he tries to do and decide everything (and he has this tendency) he will burn out and create problems in the process. I said Frank should not let Terry be a micromanager and for God's sake not to try to do this himself. To my amazement, Frank (and I tell you this in confidence) said that he was in agreement, had hesitated to appoint Terry, and that he had already talked with him about this. I am not sure I believe him, but it sure sounded convincing.

We then discussed, of all the dull subjects, the role of staff agencies. I spouted Harvard professor Michael Barzelay's "post-bureaucratic vision" of the "helping" role of staff agencies. They should be stopped—and I mean *stopped*—from interfering in every damn transaction and second-guessing every commissioner all of the time and being down in the bowels of every agency. That is what is killing initiative by people like you—purchasing, contracting, budgeting, auditing, personnel procedures. You will die a thousand deaths with this stuff, and you know it. The staff should serve the line. Frank and Terry should change the people at the top of the staff agencies and tell them in no uncertain terms that a new order is required. This is what this professor said to the new governor!

And how did he take this? Very well. He did say he hadn't thought enough about the role of the staff agencies. He asked me more about it and said he would tell Terry to come around and talk with me about how he can move the square pegs out of round holes (his phrasing) in the staff agencies. I told him he wouldn't regret putting time in on this and praised him for what sounded to me like a serious response. I guess I'm just gullible. That's why he's the governor and I'm the professor. But he did surprise me as you can see from this letter. You must be pretty surprised too.

So that's my report. Good news. Hopeful signs for a new beginning. But when the going gets tough, as John Mitchell once asked, "Will the tough get going?" I hope not. I know you won't. All the best.

Yours truly,

Dick

Dear Dick,

I can't believe your second letter. I am putting it in my safety deposit box. I hope it's for real! Thank you for your advice, which of course I like, and on behalf of all of us, for your good work with our new leader. He was full of praise for you at our first cabinet meeting. I hope he will keep in touch with you and you will reinforce these principles. I'm loving it already, but I know that there's a bumpy road ahead. Charlie sends his best.

Yours truly,

Ann

Notes

2. The Origins of "New-Style" Workfare

1. Gilbert Y. Steiner, *The State of Welfare* (Washington, D.C.: The Brookings Institution, 1971), p. 32.
2. Daniel P. Moynihan, *The Politics of a Guaranteed Income* (New York: Random House, 1973), p. 128.
3. Ibid.
4. Ibid. p. 131.
5. Martin Anderson, *Welfare* (Palo Alto: Hoover Press, 1978), p. 82.
6. Richard P. Nathan, *The Administrative Presidency* (New York: Macmillan, 1986), p. 103.
7. Ibid., p. 21.
8. Ibid., p. 19.
9. Ibid., p. 107.
10. William Safire, "Coiner's Corner," *New York Times Magazine,* July 17, 1988, p. 10.

3. Changes Under Reagan

1. Gilbert Y. Steiner, *The State of Welfare* (Washington, D.C.: The Brookings Institution, 1971), p. 1.

2. Ibid.

3. Fred Doolittle, *Ronald Reagan and Conservative Welfare Reform* (unpublished manuscript), p. 4–1.

4. Ibid., p. 4–1.

5. Ibid., p. 4–4.

6. Ibid., p. 4–11.

7. A number of studies at the time showed CWEP to be unsuccessful. Court challenges, legislative opposition, and the tendency of staff members to treat the program as voluntary rather than mandatory contributed to this situation. An analysis in 1981 by staff of the Manpower Demonstration Research Corporation concluded that the implementation of California CWEP in this period was "ineffective."

8. Lou Cannon, *Reagan* (New York: Putnam, 1982), p. 183.

9. Leonard Goodwin, *Causes and Cures of Welfare* (Lexington, Mass.: Lexington Books, 1983), p. 140.

10. Ibid.

11. Mickey Kaus, "The Work Ethic State," *New Republic* (July 7, 1986): 33.

12. Ibid., p. 32.

13. Ibid., p. 27.

14. Lawrence M. Mead, *Beyond Entitlement: The Social Obligations of Citizenship* (New York: The Free Press, 1986), p. 1.

15. Ibid., pp. 1–2.

16. Trish Peyser, "The History of the 1981 Workfare Provisions" (Princeton University senior paper, 1985), p. 9.

17. Ibid., p. 8.

18. Margaret Malone, *Work and Welfare*, 99th Cong., 2d sess. (Washington, D.C.: U.S. Government Printing Office, August 1986), p. 104. Prepared for the Subcommittee on Employment and Productivity of the Committee on Labor and Human Resources and the Subcommittee on Social Security and Income Maintenance of the Committee on Finance, United States Senate.

19. Ibid.

20. The 1981 Omnibus Budget Reconciliation Act removed the thirty dollars plus one-third of earnings deduction four months after an AFDC recipient enters employment. Later Congress partially reversed this decision. It reinstated the thirty-dollar deduction (but not the one-third of earnings deduction) on a permanent basis.

21. Malone, *Work and Welfare*, p. 106.

22. Ibid.

23. "The President's State of the Union Address, Delivered Before a Joint Session of the Congress, February 4, 1986," *Weekly Compilation of Presidential Documents* 22, no. 6 (Monday, February 10, 1986): 138.

24. Ibid.

25. Ibid.

26. "The President's State of the Union Address, Delivered Before a Joint

Session of the Congress, January 27, 1987," *Weekly Compilation of Presidential Documents* 23, no. 4 (Monday, February 2, 1987): 62.

27. Assistance in writing this section was provided by Erica Baum, Ronald Haskins, and Barbara Selfridge, although the interpretation is my responsibility alone.

28. A number of caveats were added in the House. The law requires that after nine months of participation in CWEP, workers should receive "prevailing wage rates" rather than the minimum wage. The law prohibited requiring more than twenty hours of participation per week in CWEP by AFDC participants with a child under the age of six.

29. Charles Murray, "New Welfare Bill, New Welfare Cheats," *Wall Street Journal*, October 13, 1988, sec. A, p. 22.

4. Studies of the 1981 Changes

1. Transmittal letter to Congressman Ted Weiss, January 29, 1987. United States General Accounting Office, Human Resources Division, *Work and Welfare: Current AFDC Programs and Implications for Federal Policy* (Washington, D.C.: GAO/HRD–87–34, January 1987), p. 1. Report prepared for the Chairman, Subcommittee on Intergovernmental Relations and Human Resources, Committee on Government Operations, House of Representatives.

2. Ibid., p. 49.

3. Ibid., p. 50.

4. United States General Accounting Office, Human Services Division, *Work and Welfare: Analysis of AFDC Employment Programs in Four States* (Washington, D.C.: GAO/HRD–88–33FS, January 1988), p. 21. Fact sheet prepared for the Committee on Finance, U.S. Senate.

5. Ralph Smith, *Work-related Programs for Welfare Recipients* (Washington, D.C.: Congressional Budget Office, Government Printing Office, April 1987), p. 43.

6. Barbara Goldman et al., *California: Findings from the San Diego Demonstration* (New York: Manpower Demonstration Research Corporation, March 1985), p. xxiiv.

7. Judith M. Gueron and Edward Pauly, *From Welfare to Work* (New York: Russell Sage Foundation, 1991).

5. Deciding What to Do—the Five State Programs

1. Stephen R. Rosenthal and Morris A. Shepard, "Employment and Training Choices" (unpublished case study, Boston University School of Management, 1985). According to the authors, this case study was prepared "to serve as a basis for class discussion, not to illustrate either effective or ineffective handling of a managerial situation" (p. A–1).

2. Ibid., p. A–2.

3. Ibid., p. A–4.

4. Ibid., p. A–6.

5. Ibid., p. A–5.

6. Ibid.

7. Ibid.

8. Ibid., p. A–7.

9. Personal interview with Charles Atkins, July 28, 1988.

10. Ibid.

11. Rosenthal and Shepard, "Employment and Training Choices," p. B–7.

12. *General assistance* refers to programs that aid the nonaged poor who are not covered by AFDC. In some cases, they are state programs; in others, local. Benefits are often lower than for AFDC, and there is wide variation nationally in the scope and level of aid provided, if any. The main recipients are single adults. The Pennsylvania controversy over this program—its continuance and the strong work requirement adopted—received national publicity during this period.

13. David M. Kennedy, "California Welfare Reform," Case Program, Kennedy School of Government (Cambridge, Mass.: Harvard University, 1987), p. 10. This case was written by Kennedy under the direction of Professor Jose A. Gomez-Ibanez.

14. Ibid.

15. Ibid.

16. Richard P. Nathan, *Social Science in Government* (New York: Basic Books, 1988), p. 134.

17. Thomas Martello, "Kean Unveils Reform Plan for Welfare," *Trenton Times,* January 13, 1987, p. 43.

18. "Jerseyans Strongly Endorse Governor's Welfare Reform Plan," *Star-Ledger* (Newark), March 15, 1987, p. 45.

19. "Report Rips NJ Welfare Reform," *Trentonian,* March 24, 1987, p. 32.

20. Michigan Department of Social Services, "A History of Employment and Training Programs in the Michigan Department of Social Services" (Lansing, Mich.: Office of Communications, 1990), p. 2.

21. Refer to chapter 3, pp. 13–14.

22. Michigan Department of Social Services, "A History of Employment and Training Programs," p. 9.

23. Michigan Department of Social Services, "Reducing Dependency in a Changing Economy," *The Final Report of the Governor's Blue Ribbon Commission on Welfare Reform* (Lansing, Mich.: Office of Communications, 1988), p. 45.

24. State data for MOST program (October 1987 through June 1988—monthly average) provided by Knud L. Hansen, Michigan Department of Social Services.

25. Janet C. Quint, with Barbara S. Goldman and Judith M. Gueron, *Arkansas: Interim Findings from the Arkansas WIN Demonstration Program* (New York: Manpower Demonstration Research Corporation, November 1984), pp. 5–6.

26. Daniel Friedlander et al., *Arkansas: Final Report on the WORK Program in Two Counties* (New York: Manpower Demonstration Research Corporation, September 1985), p. xv.

27. Ibid., p. xvi.

6. Program Start-Up

1. Robert D. Behn, *Leadership Counts* (Cambridge, Mass.: Harvard University Press, 1991), p. 125.

2. Angela Browne and Aaron Wildavsky, "Implementation as Exploration (1983)" in *Implementation,* ed. Jeffrey L. Pressman and Aaron Wildavsky (Berkeley: University of California Press, 1984), p. 254.

3. Robert D. Behn, "Management by Groping Along," *Journal of Policy Analysis* 7, no. 4 (Fall 1988): 656.

4. Ibid., p. 655.

5. "In Memoriam," *John F. Kennedy School of Government Bulletin* (Spring/Summer 1980): 36.

6. Behn, *Leadership Counts,* p. 73.

7. Personal interview with Howard Waddell, July 29, 1988.

8. Personal interview with Thomas Glynn, July 28, 1988.

9. Ibid.

10. Personal interview with Barbara Bourke-Tatum, July 28, 1988.

11. Thomas J. Peters and Robert H. Waterman, Jr., *In Search of Excellence* (New York: Harper and Row, 1982), pp. 321–322.

12. Behn, *Leadership Counts,* p. 118.

13. Personal interview with Jolie Bain-Pillsbury, March 3, 1989.

14. Letter from Commissioner Drew Altman to Rodney P. Frelinghuysen, chairman, Assembly Appropriations Committee, June 1, 1989.

15. Personal interview with Drew Altman, September 20, 1988.

16. Thomas J. Anton, *American Federalism and Public Policy* (Philadelphia: Temple University Press, 1989). See especially chapter 3, "The Distribution of Federal Benefits."

17. The other four were school-based youth services, reform of Medicaid, aid for the homeless under the state's AFDC emergency assistance program, and overhaul of the mental health system.

18. Personal interview with Drew Altman and Dennis Beatrice, September 20, 1988.

19. Ibid.

20. Ibid.

7. Program Operations

1. James Riccio et al., *GAIN: Early Implementation Experiences and Lessons* (New York: Manpower Demonstration Research Corporation, April 1989), p. viii.

2. The JTPA system is a federal-state program that provides training in close cooperation with business leaders in the local area. Nationally, and at the state and local levels, this system is run by labor, rather than by welfare agencies. Controversies have arisen in many areas about the claimed tendency for JTPA training programs to aid the most job-ready people, rather than the people who most needed this service.

3. Riccio et al., *GAIN: Early Implementation,* p. 52.

4. Ibid., pp. 63–64.

5. Ibid., p. iii.

6. Ibid., p. 50.

7. Ibid.

8. Ibid., p. 54.

9. Ibid.

10. Ibid., p. 56.

11. Ibid., p. 71.

12. Ibid., p. 9.

13. Ibid., p. 11.

14. Personal interview with James Riccio, June 26, 1989.

15. Riccio et al., *GAIN,* p. 114.

16. Ibid., p. 115.

17. Ibid., p. 175.

18. Ibid., p. 176.

19. Ibid., p. xix.

8. Feedback and Program Oversight

1. Herbert Kaufman, with the collaboration of Michael Couzens, *Administrative Feedback* (Washington, D.C.: The Brookings Institution, 1973), p. 65.

2. Ibid.

3. Robert D. Behn, *Leadership Counts* (Cambridge, Mass.: Harvard University Press, 1991), p. 49. (His successor said in an interview that she would keep the ten-goal system.)

4. Ibid.

5. Ibid.

6. Ibid., chapter 4, p. 6.

7. Ibid., chapter 4, p. 3.

8. Ibid.

9. Ibid., chapter 4, p. 4.

10. Ibid., chapter 4, p. 18.

11. Ibid., chapter 4, p. 15.

12. Warren T. Brookes, "The Stunning Failure of Dukakis's ET, *Wall Street Journal,* January 19, 1987, sec. A, p. 18.

13. Ibid.

14. Warren T. Brookes, "Welfare Reform: 'ET' Is the Wrong Model," *Washington Times,* December 7, 1987, sec. E, p. 3.

15. Ibid.

16. Stuart Butler and Anna Kondratas, *Out of the Poverty Trap* (New York: The Free Press, 1987), p. 145.

17. Brookes, "The Stunning Failure," p. 18.

18. Monci Jo Williams, "Is Workfare the Answer?" *Fortune* (October 17, 1986): 110.

19. Tom Morganthau et al., "Welfare: A New Drive to Clean Up the Mess," *Newsweek* (February 2, 1987): 25.

20. John Herbers, "Job Training Efforts in Massachusetts and Michigan Move Poor Off Welfare," *New York Times,* March 30, 1987, Sec. A, p. 14.

21. Milton Coleman, "New Welfare Strategy Works in Massachusetts," *Washington Post,* August 9, 1985, Sec. A, p. 3.

22. Joe Davidson, "Welfare Revised: More States Now Ask Recipients of Aid to Train and Take Jobs," *Wall Street Journal,* July 23, 1986, sec. A, p. 1.

23. Refer to chapter 3.

24. Office of Research, Planning, and Evaluation, Department of Public Welfare, *Request for Proposal for an Evaluation of Employment and Training (ET) Choices* (Commonwealth of Massachusetts: Executive Office of Human Services, August 1986), p. 3.

25. Ibid.

26. Demetra Smith Nightingale et al., "Experiences of Massachusetts ET Job Finders: Preliminary Findings" (Washington, D.C.: The Urban Institute, October 1989), p. 18. This paper was prepared for the Association of Public Policy Analysis and Management annual conference, which was held November 2–4, 1989.

27. Steve Smucker and Rose Ann Ward, "Interim Evaluation of the Michigan Opportunities Skills Training Program: Annual and Quarterly Earnings," Planning and Evaluation Division, Office of Planning Budget and Evaluation (State of Michigan: Department of Social Services, March 1989), p. 10.

9. Implementing the JOBS Program

1. Jan L. Hagen and Irene Lurie, *Implementing Jobs: Initial State Choices* (Albany: The Nelson A. Rockefeller Institute of Government, State University of New York, January 1992), p. 25.

2. Ibid.

3. Steven D. Gold and Robert Greenstein, *The States and the Poor: How Budget Decisions in 1991 Affected Low Income People* (Washington: The Center on Budget and Policy Priorities; and Albany: Center for the Study of the States, December 1991), pp. vii, viii.

4. Hagen and Lurie, *Implementing Jobs,* pp. 3–4.

5. Ibid., pp. 4–5.

6. Ibid., p. 17.

7. Ibid., p. 5.

8. Ibid., p. 17.

9. Ibid., p. 22.

10. Ibid., p. 11.

10. Why Is Welfare So Hard to Reform?

1. Material provided by Knud L. Hansen, Michigan Department of Social Services.

2. Barbara Goldman et al., *Relationship Between Earnings and Welfare Benefits For Working Recipients: Four Area Case Studies* (New York: Manpower Demonstration Research Corporation, October 1985), p. xiii.

3. Leonard Goodwin, *Do the Poor Want to Work?* (Washington, D.C.: The Brookings Institution, 1972). See especially chapter 8, pp. 112–118.

11. Changing the Way We Work in the Shadow Land

1. David Osborne and Ted Gaebler, *Reinventing Government: How the Entrepreneurial Spirit Is Transforming the Public Sector* (New York: Addison-Wesley, 1992), p. 321.

2. Hugh Heclo, *Government of Strangers* (Washington: The Brookings Institution, 1977).

3. Deborah D. Roberts, speech given at the New York State Academy for Public Administration Forum, Albany, New York, November 27, 1990.

4. Deborah D. Roberts, "The Challenge of Executive Leadership," in a paper for the National Commission on State and Local Public Service, 1991, p. 15.

5. Professional search firms charge one-quarter to one-third of the first year's annual salary for the position that is the object of the search, plus expenses.

12. Ten Lessons

1. Marian Wright Edelman, "A Call to Public Service (A Plea for Fleas)," 1987 Class Day Address, John F. Kennedy School of Government, Harvard University. Lecture published in *John F. Kennedy School of Government Bulletin* (Fall/Winter 1987): 10–13. RFP stands for Request for Proposals.

2. Jean Monnet, *Memoirs,* as quoted in Clifford Hackett, *Cautious Revolution* (New York: Praeger Press, 1990), p. 1.

3. Richard F. Elmore, "Backward Mapping: Implementation Research and Policy Decisions," in *Studying Implementation,* ed. Walter Williams (Chatham, N.J.: Chatham House, 1982), p. 24.

4. The book that was criticized is the *Administrative Presidency* (New York: Macmillan, 1986). The criticism is by Richard W. Waterman in *Presidential Influence and the Administrative State* (Knoxville: University of Tennessee Press, 1989).

Index

Designer: Susan Clark
Text: 10/12.5 Galliard
Compositor: Maple-Vail
Printer: Maple-Vail
Binder: Maple-Vail